Dr. D. K. Olukoya

Be PREPARED

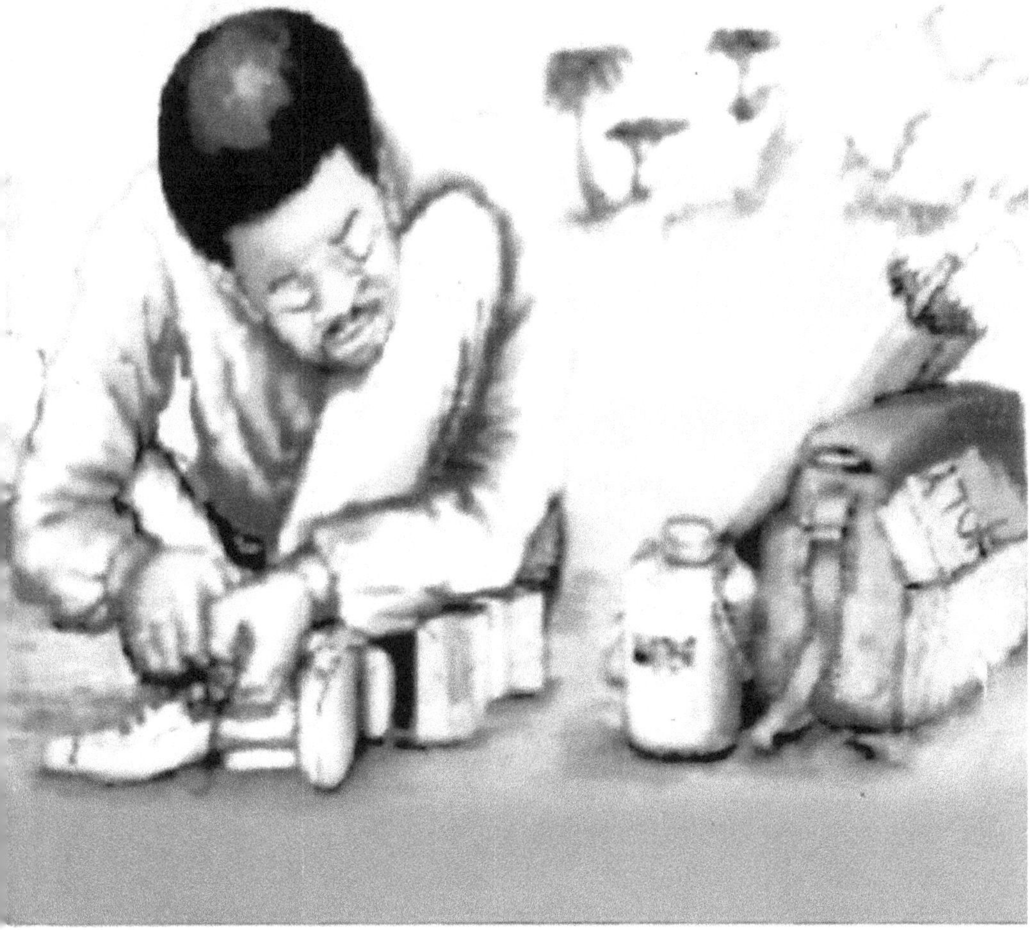

Dr. D.K. Olukoya

Be
PREPARED

© 1999
Be Prepared
Dr D. K Olukoya

A publication of TRACTS AND PUBLICATIONS GROUP
MOUNTAIN OF FIRE AND MIRACLES MINISTRIES
13, Olasimbo Street off Olumo Road.
(By UNILAG Second Gate)
Onike, Iwaya
P.O.Box 2990. Sabo, Yaba. Lagos. Nigeria.
01-868766
E-Mail: mfm@micro.com.ng
mfm@nigol.netng
Web-site: www.mountain-of-fire.com

All rights reserved. No part of this publication
may be reproduced, stored in a retrieve system,
or be transmitted, in any form, or by any means,
mechanical, electronic, photocopying or otherwise
without the prior written consent of the publisher.
It is protected under the copyright laws.

ISBN 978-9782947635

Typesetting, designing and printing at MFM PRESS
13, Olasimbo Street, Off Olumo Road, by
Unilag 2nd Gate, Onike, Yaba, Lagos, Nigeria.

Cover Illustration by: **Sis. Shade Olukoya**

Other Books published by MFM Ministries
- Students In The School Of Fear
- The Vagabond Spirit
- Power Must Change Hands
- Breakthrough Prayers For Business Professionals
- Pray Your Way To Breakthroughs (Third Edition)
- Spiritual Warfare And The Home
- Victory Over Satanic Dreams (Second Edition)
- Personal Spiritual Check-Up
- Prayers That Bring Miracles (In English, Hausa, Igbo & Yoruba Languages)
- Adura Agbayori (Yoruba Version of the Second Edition of Pray Your Way To Breakthrough)
- How To Obtain Personal Deliverance (Second Edition)
- Power Against Local Wickedness
- Brokenness
- Let God Answer By Fire (In English, French, Hausa, Igbo and Yoruba languages)
- Release From Destructive Covenants
- PRIER JUSQUEA REMPORTER LA VICTOIRE (French Edition of Pray Your Way To Breakthroughs)
- Power Against Spiritual Terrorists
- Deliverance of The Head
- Revoking Evil Decrees
- The Great Deliverance
- Wealth Must Change Hands
- Limiting God
- Power Against Coffin Spirits
- Satanic Diversion of The Black Race
- Prayers To Mount Up With Wings As Eagles (In English, French, Hausa, Igbo and Yoruba Languages)
- Holy Cry
- Power Against Destiny Quenchers
- Prayer Rain
- Holy Fever
- The Fire of Revival

This and other publications of MFM Ministries can be obtained from:
MFM BOOKS HOP 13, Olasimbo Street, off Olumo Road,
by Unilag 2nd Gate,
Onike, Yaba, Lagos, Nigeria.
Or any other leading Christian bookstores

TABLE OF CONTENT

Chapter One
THE GREAT EIGHT QUESTIONS 5

Chapter Two
THE BIG PREPARATION 23

Chapter Three
OCCUPY TILL I COME 38

Chapter Four
SHORT BED AND NARROW BLANKET 52

Chapter Five
THE RAPTURE 69

Chapter Six
THE COMING GREAT EVENT 84

Chapter Seven
THE WHITE THRONE JUDGEMENT 105

Chapter 1

The Great Eight Questions

It is not difficult to know that only very few people think. While thinking may look quite natural, it is a very hard work and sometimes a very dangerous assignment. Only very few people do serious thinking, and even fewer people engage in serious meditation. It is a fact that people do not really settle down to think about the world in which they found themselves and about life in general. That is why the Bible says, "*O that they are wise, they would consider their end.*" Even many do not think about their own personal life, and the devil ensures that people waste time thinking about unimportant things. This is why you have to ask yourselves the following eight questions:

1. Where do I come from?
2. Who am I?
3. Why am I here?

4. What happens when I die?
5. Where am I now?
6. What do I see?
7. When the Son of Man comes, shall He find faith in me?
8. Will I be made whole?

If as a Christian, you have never really thought of these questions or meditated on them, then you need serious prayers, because they are indeed serious eternal issues. Let us consider them one after the other.

1. WHERE DO I COME FROM?
Most people have not bothered to ask themselves where they came from. Have you ever thought of that? Where is your origin? It is a known fact that many people do not think of their roots. It is certain that somebody who does not know where he is coming from, would not know what he wants in this life and hereafter. If your answer to the question, "Where do you come from," is "I don't know," that is quite unsatisfactory. You must know your origin. The Bible makes it very clear that God created you and I. Psalms 8: 4 - 6 says:
"What is man, that thou art mindful of him? And the son of man that thou visitest him? For thou has made him a little lower than

Be Prepared

The angels and hast crowned him with glory and honour. Thou modest him to have dominion over the works of thy hands, thou hast put all things under his feet."

This tells us that man was created by God, but a time came when he lost all the glory of God, and got into trouble. So, no matter how great man is, his physical body is dust. The Lord told him, **"Dust thou art and unto the dust thou shalt return."** It is only the spirit of man that goes back to God. So, the next time you feel like boasting, remember, "Dust thou art and unto the dust thou shall return." Let it be very clear in your spirit, that whether a person is rich or poor, unto dust shall the person return. We came from God and that is where we must compulsorily go back to unless we are rebels and do not want to go back to Him.

2. WHO AM I?
This is a question of identity. You may be putting yourself into trouble if you are ignorant of your identity. If for example, you are walking along the street and a policeman asks you to identify yourself, your identity card which reveals who you are must be produced. Failure to produce an authentic identity card in such a situation is to court trouble.

The Bible tells us that man is made in the image of God. He is a free, rational person and quite different from animals. The Bible says that each person is a spirit living in a body and having a soul. God made the man and the woman, but because they both sinned, they were cursed. We are all made in the image of God, but unfortunately, that image has been defaced and spoilt, and man is lost. He also has no hope in this world or even the next. Man is a lost soul walking about in the wilderness and it is only by giving his life to Christ that he can find his way out. The question of identity is so important that apostles of old were asked questions that pertained to their identities. In John 1: 22, John the Baptist was queried by the Jews. They were in doubt about the identity of John, and therefore asked him; **"Who art thou, that we may give an answer to them that sent us."** John the Baptist then answered: **"I am the voice of one crying in the wilderness. Make straight the way of the Lord, as said the prophet Esaias."**

God has a general purpose for all of us, but you must know who you are. If you do not know who you are, then you are opening your door to problems. The lesson on identity is an important one. Jacob learnt that lesson. He knew that by his identity, he was not in the place of blessing. If you have read Genesis 27, you will discover how he used foul means to get his brother's blessing. He got it by claiming his brother's identity.

Be Prepared

Let this be clear in your spirit that one of satan's most effective devices is to get people to doubt their own identities. He did it to Jesus, so he can do it to anybody. He told Jesus, "If you are the son of God, command these stones to become bread." He did not stop at that, he again told Jesus that if he was the son of God, he should cast himself down. When Jesus was on the cross, satan, came again to tempt Him. He told Jesus that if He was truly the son of God, He should come down from the cross. It is therefore possible for the devil to challenge you by saying, if you are truly a child of God, you should not be suffering.

That is why as a believer, you should not confess negatively. "I am not worthy, I am worn out, I am unfit" etc, could be your old identity tags, but once you have given your life to Jesus and if by the grace of God, you are living the kind of life God wants you to live, you should not call yourself strange names again. If you still do, it means you do not know who you are. The prodigal son was bad, but at a stage, he came to himself and remembered who he was. He remembered that he was a son and not a slave. So, you too must remember who you are. When Jesus was in the world, He did not hide His identity. He identified Himself as the light and as the bread of life.

The Bible tells us what our identity is. It says that we are the branches, new creatures, not refurbished ones. The Bible says that we are God's workmanship, we are more than conquerors and our lives are hid in Christ. All these point to our collective identity and you must know them. Do not be like Peter who was released from jail and did not know.

The day you know that you belong to God, your Creator, that day, you will begin to live a victorious life. At this juncture, I would like you to pray this way: "O Lord, show me who I am in the spirit, O Lord, open my understanding, in the name of Jesus."

It was possible for Elijah to do exploits for the Lord because he realised his position in Jesus. He knew his identity early enough. Who are you then in the spiritual scale of the Almighty: God? What can you use to identify yourself in the spirit. Pleas pray again that the garment of ignorance should be roasted, it the name of Jesus.

3. WHY AM I HERE?
What is your purpose on earth? God has put all of us here on earth for a purpose. Generally, God wants us to know Him and to fellowship with Him. He wants us to recover all that we have lost through Adam.

Be Prepared

God wants us to experience His grace in our lives. We are here because of what Jesus did at Calvary. We are here so that others can learn from our lives, from the testimony of what Jesus did for us, and what He can also do for them. We are here too to do battle with satan. The question is, what is your own purpose as an individual? Have you found out from the Lord? A wasted life is a life without a purpose. Until your purpose for living is discovered, life may have no meaning to you. Your reason for being here on earth provides the key to your existence. These things must be clear in your spirit. You cannot live your life on experiment or on trial and error basis.

Life is so short that you cannot experiment with it. You cannot afford to live on assumption. Pray again like this: "O Lord, make my purpose for living plain before my eyes, I bind every spirit of aimlessness." You must know this fact, that the spirit of this age is the spirit of aimlessness. In everything you do in life, you must have a purpose for it, be it marriage, business, etc. The reason there is so much confusion now is that people are outside God's purpose for their lives. They are busy pursuing their own little dreams. The carpenter is busy doing the driving job and the painter is hell-bent on flying the aircraft. When this happens, a person's purpose is defeated, and things wouldn't work the way they should.

4. WHAT HAPPENS WHEN I DIE?

The Bible answers this question. It paints the picture of two places, and the contrast between them is frightening. The world we are in now is at present satan's world. Our kingdom, will overcome this one. Jesus says clearly that when men die, they go to either of two places, heaven or hell. The Bible's graphic description of these two places makes the contrast very clear. It is given to man to die only once, after that judgement. It is better for a person not to be born at all than for him to end up in hell fire. The Bible makes us to realise that when the rich man died, he found himself in hell fire, while Lazarus too died and found himself in the bosom of Abraham. Talk to the Lord in prayer like this: "Anything that will take me to hell fire, get out of my life now, in the name of Jesus."

5. WHERE AM I NOW?

Genesis 3: 9- 10 says, *"And the Lord God called unto Adam and said unto him, where art thou. And he said, I heard thy voice in the garden, and I was afraid because I was naked: and I hid myself.*

Where are you? What an interesting question. Was it that God did not know where Adam was? God asked that

Be Prepared

When God asks you where you are? The meaning is, where is your spiritual location in Him. What do you weigh in His balance? Nebuchadnezzar was a very great king and there has never been a kingdom so great in splendour and might and glory like the kingdom of Babylon that Nebuchadnezzar was heading. But God dealt with him when he got too proud. God sent him into the bush and humbled him completely. He ate leaves like animals. Whatever you are doing, whether good or bad; God has His weighing balance. If God were to put you in His scales at this moment, where you are will determine your balance on that scale. A lot of people's weight are equal to zero. Ask yourself, "Where am I in the spiritual scale of the Almighty?" If you love yourself, make this declaration: "I refuse to be used as a bad example in the name of Jesus." When you are not where you should be, you can become an easy target for the enemy. What is your spiritual temperature?

Perhaps the Lord has searched for you amongst divine dreamers, visionaries, prophets etc, and your name was not in any of these places. Then; suddenly the devil shouts, God, I have his name in my own evil books! I have her name in my own terrible records." So the voice of the Lord is ringing out to you today loud and clear saying, "Where are you?"

A lot of spiritually lame people come to church. Their gifts of

Be Prepared

question because Adam was no longer in the right place. He had left where God wanted him to be. Because Adam was in the wrong place, God changed his original intention for him. He threw him out of the garden and put an angel with the sword of fire at the gate, so that the man would not be able to find his way back there. Know this beloved, when you depart from the path of God for your life, a 40 - day journey will take 40 years. It is a pity that so many people have never" really found out God's plans for their lives. If you are one of such people, God is asking you at this moment: Where are you? Some have discovered God's plans for their lives, but have abandoned the plans after listening to people of the world. I do hope you know that money, education and material possessions are not signs that you are enjoying God's blessing. The sign can only be seen in you when you are at the center of God's will.

Are you at the center of God's will for you life, or are you like David who stayed at home while others were fighting, or Peter who was warming himself at the enemy's fire? No wonder then, that Peter at a point in time started to follow the Lord from afar. Are you in the wrong place in your career, business or spiritual life? When you are in the wrong place, you cannot receive God's blessings. All that you can get are crumbs here and there. You will not have correct fellowship with the Lord and this will make you an easy target for the devil.

vision have disappeared. They were on fire before, but now they have become cold. We have spiritually deaf and dumb people too in large numbers in many churches today. They do not hear from the Lord, neither do they see any vision. They do not comprehend anything. It is not surprising at all that such people invest even in wrong places in the physical world. Your answer to this question is very important. Where are you? Belteshazzar eventually knew where he was. God told him that He had finished the arithmetic of his kingdom and had weighed it and found him wanting.

Please close your eyes and talk to the Lord about yourself this way: "Set my life on fire for you, and bury all my lukewarmness, in the name of Jesus." Look inward, are you still being harassed by, the spirit of fear. If the kind of things that used to put fears into your life are still doing so now, it shows that you have not grown up at all. Perhaps, your faith is still as rudimentary as when you just believed. Perhaps, your knowledge of God is so hazy that you never used the name or Jesus to defeat any power of the enemy in your life. Perhaps you have been a believer for one year or two and you cannot differentiate between the voice of the Holy Spirit, your voice and the devil's, then the solution is to seek for help, and not to console yourself by saying that you are better than someone else.

6. WHAT DO YOU SEE?

Let us go to the book of Jeremiah. The Lord asked Jeremiah another interesting question in Jeremiah 1: 4-14. *"Then the word of the Lord came unto me saying, before I formed thee in the belly, I knew thee and before thou comest forth out of the womb, I sanctified thee, and I ordained thee a prophet unto the nations. Then said I, Ah, Lord, God behold, I cannot speak for I am a child. But the Lord said unto me, say not, I am a child: for thou shalt go to all that I shall send thee, and whatsoever I command thee thou shalt speak. Be not afraid of their faces: for I am with thee to deliver thee, saith the Lord. Then the Lord put forth his hand, and touched my mouth. And the Lord said unto me, Behold, I have put my words in thy mouth. See, I have this day set thee over the nations and, over the kingdoms, to root out, and to pull down, and to destroy and to throw down, to build and to plant. Moreover the word of the Lord came unto me, saying, Jeremiah, what seest thou? And I said, I see a rod of an almond tree. Then said the Lord unto me, Thou hast well seen; for I will hasten my word to perform it. And the word of the Lord came unto me the second time, saying, What seest thou? And I said, I see a seething pot; and the face thereof is toward the north. Then the Lord said unto, me, out of the North an evil shall break forth upon all the inhabitants of theland."*

So I ask you the same question, what do you see? Was it that the Lord did not know what Jeremiah saw. Why was He asking that question? The Lord may be showing you the vision of your life and you have not seen it. Your spiritual vision may have what is called, "spiritual cataract" which can prevent you from seeing what the Lord wants you to see. If you have made up your mind on what you want to do, before you come to the Lord, and say, "O Lord, show me the way." You can be rest assured that you will not see anything. This is because you have already made up your mind on what to do before coming to the Lord.

Beloved, perhaps you are without a vision or plan for your Christian life, you really need to pray. The voice of the Lord is asking you, "What do you see?" God never calls a meeting for entertainment. At the Mountain of Fire and Miracles Ministries, for example, there is no room for satanic entertainment. There are lots of entertainment churches all around for those who want to be entertained. God has a serious purpose for bringing people to fellowship at MFM. God has His own distinctive purpose and has no useless exercise. Even if the whole world is aimless and purposeless, God has a purpose for everything He does. God believes in man so much that He invested His son into it. And by so doing, He expects returns from man. If I may ask you this question,

Do you know for sure what is happening to you? What stage are you in the history of your life? Have you seen the personal vision God has for you?

Do you know your purpose in life? If you don't know the vision of God for your life, then you will not be able to plan. God does not experiment. He knows what He is doing. So, the earlier you find out what He wants you to do and begin to do it, the better. God is called the Alpha and the Omega because before He starts a thing, He has completed it. God never starts a thing without finishing it. God was determined that Jesus was to be born and that He would die to redeem man. All these were clear in His mind before He started to look for Mary who would deliver the child. Why did God conceive you?

Do not be one of those people getting confused or prospering in the wrong things. The fact that what you are doing now is prospering does not mean that it is right. Please close your eyes and pray seriously to the Lord this way, **"Open my eyes to see your purpose for my life, in the name of Jesus."** There are various ways to recognise those people who do not have visions for their lives. They will prophesy and disobey the prophecy. They will be the ones to say, "My servant, my servant, I want, to use you mightily." But they would be the same people who gave the prophecy that will be committing sin. They always move from one business to another without making any headway. They do not really know what God wants them to do. They choose their spouses through physical observations. They receive direct messages from the Lord and then put them aside. They want to lead others but do not want to be led. Any small failure they experience, they would get discouraged. These are the people without vision. But for somebody who knows what he has seen, all the discouragement and failures on the way, are nothing but fertilizers.

Those without vision are the ones who see men looking like trees. They criticize others concerning sins which they themselves commit. They do not know whether what they are hearing is from God or the devil. There are many of them in the churches agitating for church posts. Some find it hard to serve the Lord unless they are in leadership position. Many of us dream very well, but how many of us know what we are dreaming about? Have you got to that level when you will be having a dream and right there in the dream you will be asking the Lord what the dream is all about? Not that you will wake up confused, and then start praying for the meaning of the dream for three months without an answer? No, you have to be better than that.

7. WHEN THE SON OF MAN COMETH, SHALL HE FIND FAITH IN ME?

This is found in Luke 18 : 7- 8: *"And shalt not God avenge His own elect which cry day and night unto Him, though He bear long with them? I tell you that he will avenge them speedily. Nevertheless when the son of man cometh, shall he find faith on earth?"* Let us make that question personal. When the Son of man comes, shalt He find faith in you and I? You can see that Jesus never answered that question. He just asked and it is left for you and I to answer the question in our hearts.

The dangers of the last days have caught up with many Christians. Supposing He comes today, since He may come, at anytime, will He still find faith in your heart?

8. WILL I BE MADE WHOLE?

The last question is found in John 5:6. Jesus directed his question to a man who did not know Him. The man was afflicted by the spirit of infirmity, *"When Jesus saw him lie, and knew that he had been now a long time ill that case, he saith unto him, wilt thou be made whole?* Will you be made whole too? If you say yes, I will like the Lord to make me whole, do you know He can do so this moment? If you are happy and satisfied with the level you are now, you will never progress.

But when you know that God is calling you to climb higher, then you will dedicate yourself the more. You will be more committed, more prayerful and you will increase your Bible reading time, your prayer time, and your witnessing time. The Lord will help you, in Jesus name. God is interested in our total life. He is interested in how well we are doing.

Do you know the Biblical truth that a thousand years in His sight is like a passing night? God has His own arithmetic. The question is what do you weigh in His balance? How are you on His Spiritual scale now? Are you a thermostat Christian or a thermometer Christian. A thermometer Christian is the type that the environment determines his temperature. While a thermostat Christian will make the environment to conform to him. He is not moved by what is happening around Him. What God needs first is our spirit man. Any fire that enters the spirit is sufficient to melt all problems. How can fire enter into the spirit when the spirit is already blocked? What adjustment has God been asking you to make in your life? Has He been asking you to correct your thinking, dressing, speech, prayer life or Bible reading? Rise up today and do what the Lord wants you to do. Do not behave like a hypocrite because the hope of the hypocrites shall perish. If the trumpet shall utter an uncertain sound, the Bible says,

Be Prepared

"Who shall prepare for battle?". What kind of fruit is your life bearing? Is your life bearing positive fruits that will attract people to the Lord or fruits that will throw people down to the bottom of hell fire? You are going to open your mouth and pray the following prayer points aggressively with your right hand on your chest.

PRAYER POINTS

1. I refuse to let sin have dominion over me, in the name of Jesus.

2. I bind you spirit of anger, in the name of Jesus.

3. Lord, come into my heart in a different way, in the name of Jesus.

4. Every tree of spiritual failure be uprooted, in the name of Jesus.

Chapter 2

The Big Preparation

From what is happening around us these days, we know that the second coming of the Lord is at hand and these are more than sufficient to convince us that those things we have heard about but sounded unbelievable will surely come to pass. You can be sure that you are watching the signs of the end times. Therefore, you must be wary of the coming of the Lord and join in the big preparation. The time to start is now. The Lord will open your understanding as you read on. Let us look at some scriptures on the Lord's second coming. Amos 4 : 12 says,

"Therefore thus will I do unto thee, O Israel: and because I will do this unto thee, prepare to meet thy God, O Israel."
Matthew 24 : 44 too says, *"Therefore, be ye also ready: (which means be prepared) for in such an hour as ye think*

not, the Son of man cometh." Luke 14 : 28 - 32 has this to say, "For which of you, intending to build a tower, sitteth not down first and counteth the cost, whether he has sufficient to finish it? Lest haply, after he hath laid the foundation, and is not able to finish it, all that behold it begin to mock him; saying, this man began to build and was not able to finish. Or what king going to make war against another king, sitteth not down first, and consulted whether he be able with ten thousand to meet him that cometh with twenty thousand? Or else, while the other is yet a great way off, he sendeth an ambassage and desireth conditions of peace."

GOD IS A GOD OF PREPARATION

All these three passages above convey the same message; that all of us must be prepared to meet God. When you study those passages closely, you will easily discover that God is a God of preparation. The Bible is replete with many instances to establish this fact. Before Jesus went to any city, He first of all sent His disciples there to prepare ahead of Him. Even John the Baptist was sent as a preparation because he was said to be the voice of the one crying in the wilderness, "Prepare ye the way of the Lord, make His path straight" Noah spent 120 years preparing the Ark. People laughed him to scorn but he continued, and for 120 years he was getting ready. The Bible says that eyes have not seen,

Be Prepared

ears have not heard, neither has it come into the mind of man what God has prepared for His own people. The popular passage in John 14:1-2 says, *"Let not your heart be troubled, ye believe in God, believe also in me. In my father's house are many mansions. If it were not so, I would have told you. I go to prepare a place for you."*

And in Matthew also, you will find that God also prepared hell fire for the devil and his angels and not for you and I. Any believer that therefore finds his way to hell fire is a trespasser, because he is not supposed to be there. That place is not prepared for us.

When God makes His preparations, He does it well. For instance, the visitation of the Holy Ghost baptism on the 120 apostles. The apostles for ten days, were in the upper room preparing. But before then, they were busy arguing on who was going to be what. So God used those ten days to train them. When God finished with them, they were no longer worried about who was going to be what. They became more worried about how to preach the gospel. God is therefore a God of preparation. God who prepared the people of old, is now talking to you and I, that we too must be prepared.

During a particular church service, a man who came singing and rejoicing, suddenly collapsed. Before anyone could say Jesus is Lord, he was stone dead. In order not to cause any further uproar, a prayer point was called, and the man was taken to the back of the church. By the time the church had prayed for about an hour, the man opened his eyes and asked if there was a wedding ceremony in that church the previous day. Those that prayed for him answered in the affirmative. He then informed them that God took him to heaven during the short time he died and there, he saw the newly wedded couple. Initially, no one took him serious, but before the end of the service, news came that the newly - wedded couple in question, that went on honeymoon, had an accident and were both dead. It was only then that they believed him. The main message the man was telling everyone was the need for them to get ready to meet their Lord, that heaven is real and God's judgment is certain. God does not carry out His judgment without warning people.

The Bible is filled with prophecies, promises, and pronouncements concerning that day. It will be a day of reckoning, you and I must prepare for that day. Why do we need to prepare for the day when our Lord would come? The answer is not farfetched. The meeting cannot be cancelled because it is certain.

Be Prepared

There is no amount of argument here on earth that can abort it. The meeting with God is unavoidable. We have a choice as to how to meet God; but we have no choice as far as meeting Him is concerned. And the time of the meeting too is unknown to man, for Matthew 24: 36 says, **"But of that day and hour knoweth no man, no, not even the angel of heaven but my Father only."** The uncertainty of the time, coupled with the certainty of the meeting, makes it urgent for you and I to prepare. You cannot be prepared to meet God in a sinful condition. If you are living in any known sin, like fornication, drunkenness, anger, pride, etc, then you are not making the correct preparation for this meeting with God which will come suddenly. Ecclesiastes 9:12 says, **"For man also knoweth not his time, as the fishes that are taken in an evil net, and as the birds that are caught in the snare, so are the sons of men snared in an evil time, when it falleth suddenly upon them."**

By the time He comes, whoever is not ready will have no room for any further preparation. No one reading this message has a good reason for not preparing to meet God. God will not accept any excuse from you for your unpreparedness. If the Lord calls you home now, there will be no explanation or excuse. Will you say you didn't know about the Bible? Or you did not hear about Jesus? Or you did not know how to pray fire prayers? What will be your excuse for not preparing?

This reminds me of some negro praise worship song we used to sing in those days. It says, "It is nobody's fault but mine, if I die, and my soul gets lost; it's nobody's fault but mine. Because my mother taught me how to pray, so if I die, and my soul gets lost, it is nobody's fault" We are living in the days of great revival and many more people are getting born again now. Any crowd that you have ever seen in your life will be just nothing compared to the crowd explosion of the last meeting day. Daniel saw hundreds of thousands of people. John said he saw a multitude of people which no man could number.

If the Bible says no man can number anything, it means the worldly computer too cannot number it. The man called Adolf Hiltler had no time to attend any religious meetings, He did not attend any church, but he would be at that meeting. Similarly, all those that never believed in the existence of God would be summoned to that great meeting. When some come to revival meetings, they will refuse to close their eyes. Some refuse to pray, or bow to the Lord. Some Christians hate kneeling down to pray. Some outrightly hate prayer meetings and many Christians are making the hearts of their pastors to bleed by being absent from meetings they ought to attend. This attitude shows unseriousness and lack of preparation for that day. It is

Be Prepared

possible to get late to church, get late for appointments or even cancel appointments here on earth. But at that particular meeting, nobody will come late. Everyone will be there on time. Whether people know how to pray or not, they will pray. The sad thing is that such prayers would be of no use then just like the prayers of the rich man who refused to attend to Lazarus on earth. I pray that you will not pray when it is too late, in Jesus name.

Every tongue shall be loosed, and they will talk. Ministers and presidents will confess Jesus as Lord. The Bible says that the scripture cannot be broken, hence what is in Romans 14 : 11 must compulsorily come to pass. It says, **"For it is written, As I live, saith the Lord, every knee shall bow to me, and every tongue shall confess to God."**

Sometime ago, at a particular prayer meeting, a girl who was leading praise worship came to me after the meeting, asking me to help her. She broke down in tears and said that she had aborted ten good times and she had the last one the previous week to that time. I wondered why a person leading praise worship in the church could do such a thing. But the truth is that, many still live and died in their sins like that, unless they come to themselves and repent. Do not allow the enemy to deceive you by telling you that nobody is seeing you. There is an all seeing eye, the eye that can bend into corners to see everybody. Take a look at your spiritual life.

If every believer were to be praying the way you do, or studying their Bible the way you do, then there will be no revival fire. Examine yourself. You may embrace any religion now, but on that day, you will acknowledge Jesus as Lord. It will be very sad if all those who are pretending to be godly now by attending church services eventually find themselves in the same place with the devil. Such people will suffer most in hell fire. This is why we must be serious with what we are doing.

Beloved, you must prepare now. God is a God of preparation and He expects us to prepare to meet Him. Are you really preparing to meet God? It is easier to prepare for miracles and deliverance than to prepare for heaven. Do not be deceived, whatsoever will not make you qualify for heaven, will also steal your miracle. It is a vicious circle. Everyone of us would give detailed account of our works. A Christian brother died at an unripe age of 26. This made the other brethren in the church very sad. But as they were about to bury him, God opened the eyes of one woman of God there and she saw a conversation going on between the dead brother and an old woman who was also a member of that church. The brother was telling the old woman that it was not her fault to have succeeded in killing him, that it was due to his sin. The woman boastfully responded that all other brothers and sisters still living in sin and hypocrisy in that church would be eliminated like him. The truth is that, this brother would not have become a prey to his enemies if he had not dipped his hands into sin.

Remember that you are going to give account of everything you did here on earth. You will account for every idle word, back biting, gossiping and demonic advertisement you have made. If you are backbiting or gossiping, then you are a demonic advertiser. You are doing the job of the devil for him. Many are quick to confess other people's sin. They confess the sin of the pastor, instead of praying for him. They confess the sins of the elders, and forget about theirs. You too will give account of everything you have done, whether good or bad. Everybody must appear at the judgement seat of Christ. Some people hate the truth, but the funny thing about the truth is that it is very stubborn. You can do whatever you can to suppress it, it will rise up again. Even if you build up your lies for 25 years, in one second, the truth will catch up with it.

So many people are busy deceiving themselves, saying that they are attending their family church. That family church could as well be called the family coffin because these places have not succeeded in changing their lives for better. Any believer still living in sin is just causing more problems for his church. Luke 12:2 says, **"For there is nothing covered that will not be revealed, neither hid that shall not be known"**.

The immorality you commit with your boss in the office is not covered. The alcohol in your fridge is not covered. The clever smoking of cigarette and then licking of peppermint thereafter, gossiping and all cleverly concealed sins are not covered, God sees them. The fake holiness you exhibit is not covered. What some people understand to be holiness is suppressed anger, suppressed fornication etc while the real thing is still there, breathing inside.

A time is coming when the secret of all hearts shall be made bare. We shall all see it. There is nothing covered that shall not be revealed, neither hid, that shall not be known. Therefore, whatsoever you are saying in secret shall be heard in the open and proclaimed upon house tops. Would you like what you're saying in secret to be amplified over the microphone to the whole world?

Be Prepared

Remember this fact always, that the Lord can hear what you think. Every secret thing would be made public for everybody to hear. When you know that what you are going to say is a sin, why don't you just shut your mouth and let that thought die stillborn, instead of asking for forgiveness before uttering the sinful statement? It is true that your mouth belongs to you, but you cannot afford to say whatever you want with it. If you do, God will definitely mete adequate punishment to you. Beloved, please know this from today that transgression of the law is a sickness. It contaminates the whole being.

Whenever you are living in sin, you will have a cloud covering your face from seeing God. When you are living in sin, there will be a binding power which will hold you from receiving spiritual benefits. Living in sin is tantamount to writing letters to eaters of peace and health.

The Bible says that your sins shall find you out. Though, hands join hands, no sinner would go unpunished. It will be disastrous beloved, to be a servant of sin at that glorious gathering. You will definitely not have excuses to give to God at the meeting of reckoning. You cannot wish that your sins be last or stolen, it is not possible. You may keep your own records and afterwards lose them. I have in fact seen

Somebody who lost his birthday certificate, school certificate, and his degree certificate all at once. But God will not lose His own records. The position in which you are caught is the position in which you will be judged.

We all have the glorious appointment to keep. It is one appointment that nobody will miss. I once saw a man who came late for his wedding and because the pastor kept to time, the wedding services started without the bridegroom in attendance. But let me assure you now that nobody will come late to that inevitable meeting.

You may be wandering where God keeps all these records in heaven. Who invented shorthand? It is a man. So, if man can write shorthand, make compact discs, and put a whole library inside one computer, then God can keep any record. Any reasonable man must know that there will be a day of reckoning. But a lot of people try not to think about that kind of thing or read anything concerning it. It is like they have made up their minds and do not want to know any fact about the great meeting.

God also has a speedometer. That speedometer is your memory. An international report says that when a person learns a thing, an average of six out of seven of it is forgotten. But in that meeting, everybody will have perfect memory, to remember everything that you have done.

There was an interesting story of a man who fell into a river. As he was drowning, every sin he had ever committed flashed before his face within that twinkle of an eye. After he was rescued, he decided that he was going to live a righteous life till Jesus comes. A time is coming when the cross would be changed to a sword and will judge everyone on that day. On that great meeting day, there will be no earth, moon, stars, calendars or clocks. There will be daylight throughout. It is important to pray beloved, that the day does not catch us unawares. The Bible says, "Let him that thinketh he standeth take heed, lest he fall." If you are walking about with some false confidence, then you will be caught unawares on that great meting day. Yes, God will not allow a single sinner to enter into heaven to live with His saints.

If God could cast the angels that sinned into fire, then you and I should be wary of the lives we live. Are you really prepared? I am not asking you if you have your name in the church register or how long you have been attending the church or how long ago you gave your life to Christ. These are irrelevant! The question is, are you prepared? The book of life will be opened and people will be judged from what is written in it. It does not matter whether you believe there is hell fire or not. The Bible remains true any day. If as a contractor you use inferior material to execute your contracts, you are not preparing to meet God. All the politicians that promise one thing and do something else, are not preparing to meet God.

All the tomato sellers that put rotten ones beneath are not prepared to see God. Men who make and drink alcohol and criticise everybody around are not ready to meet God. One thing is certain, God is the inevitable judge on the day of reckoning.

Beloved, be prepared!

PRAYER POINTS

1. Thank God for your redemption.

2. Confess your sins before the Lord and ask for forgiveness.

3. Father Lord, establish me in every good work, in Jesus name.

4. Spirit of God, help and increase me in the knowledge, of God, in Jesus name.

5. Father Lord, let your word have free course in my life, in Jesus' name.

6. Father Lord, let whatever hates the gospel in my life be frustrated, in Jesus name.

Chapter 3

Occupy Till I Come

The title of this message is taken from Luke 19: 13. It says, "...Occupy till I come." It is a direct order from the Lord. Since you believed in the Lord, are you occupying according to His instruction? Perhaps, you have discarded the idea of watching and waiting for His second coming. What is your present position in the register of God? The Lord's order should be taken seriously.

What must you do to occupy till He comes? The answer to this and other questions you may wish to ask, are provided in this message. Please open your heart and let the Lord bless you with this message. Let us look at an interesting scripture in Luke 19: 12 - 26 which says,
"He said therefore, a certain nobleman went into a far country to receive for himself a kingdom, and to return. And he called

Be Prepared

his ten servants, and delivered them ten pounds, and said unto them, Occupy till I come. But his citizens hated him, saying, We will not have this man to reign over us. And it came to pass, that when he was returned, having received the kingdom, then he commanded these servants to be called unto him, to whom he had given the money, that he might know how much every man had gained by trading. Then came the first, saying, Lord, thy pound hath gained ten pounds. And he said unto him, well, thou good servant: because thou hast been faithful in a very little, have thou authority over ten cities. And the second came saying, Lord, thy pound hath gained five pounds. And he said likewise to him, Be thou also over five cities. And another came, saying, Lord, behold, here is thy pound, which I have kept laid up in a napkin: For I feared thee, because thou art an austere man: thou takest up that thou layedst not down, and reapest that thou didst not sow. And he saith unto him, out of thine own mouth will I judge thee, thou wicked servant. Thou knewest that I was an austere man, taking up that I laid not down, and reaping that I did not sow. Wherefore then gavest not thou my money into the bank, that at my coming I might have required mine own with usury? And he said unto them that stood by, take from him the pound, and give it to him that hath ten pounds. (And they said unto him, Lord, he hath ten pounds.) For I say unto you, that unto every one which hath shall be given; and from him that hath not, even that he hath shall be taken away from him."

Now we have read the parable of our Lord Jesus Christ, telling us to occupy till He comes. In this parable, Jesus represents the noble man who went to take a kingdom and so gave money to His servants to trade with. Some made profit while one did not. Jesus was angry with the lazy servant. The truth is that Jesus is coming again.

The way God reasons is different from the way we reason. After all, He says, "My thoughts are not your thoughts, neither are my ways your ways." As a matter of fact, as the heavens are far away from the earth, so are God's ways and thoughts far from ours. For example, God's law of prosperity demands that whosoever wants to prosper must first give and thereafter he shall be given. However, in contrast to this, man's laws require one to think of himself alone, and to store as much as possible for himself. God's law of faith says, "Believe, then you will see." But man's law says that seeing is believing. The Bible says, "Love your enemies," but man says, "Hate and destroy them."

Many people believe that death is the end of everything. But the Bible says that, *"It is given unto man to die once, after that, judgement."* (Heb. 9:27) People often say that there are many doors or many ways to God. They believe therefore that God could be reached through other deities, objects or even through some human beings. But in total contrast to that erroneous belief, Jesus says the following in John 14: 6: **"I am the way, the truth and the life and no one cometh unto the Father, but by me."** Likewise, many people which come to church do not believe that Jesus is coming back again. II Peter 3: 3 - 4 says,

"Knowing this first, that there shall come in the last days scoffers, walking after their own lusts, and saying, where is the promise of his coming? For since the fathers fell asleep, all things continue as they were from the beginning of the creation."

Many people often say that since Jesus has not come till now, He may probably not come again. However, the Bible's position on the second coming of Jesus Christ is made explicit in II Peter 3 : 9 - 11 which says,

"The Lord is not slack concerning His promise as some men count slackness; but is long suffering to us-ward, not willing that any should perish, but that all should come to repentance. But the day of the Lord will come as a thief in the night in which the heavens shall pass away with great noise, and the elements shall melt with fervent heat, the earth also and the works that are therein shall be burned up. Seeing then that all these things

shall be dissolved, what manner of persons ought ye to be in all holy conversation and godliness."

The truth is that man is sitting on a time bomb which is about to explode. It is clear that nobody brought anything into this world and it is quite certain that nobody will take anything out of it. So, holding on to the temporal and earthly things that will soon pass away is not sensible at all. If you still do not make heaven after all the word of God you heard, deliverance, baptism in the Holy Spirit, and earth shaking prayers, then, you have succeeded in wasting all of your life and time. It would have been better if you never attended any church and spent your life and time doing your own wish.

Anything you achieved on earth is in vain, if you are not able to reign with Christ. If a cripple receives healing and begins to walk about, but is not able to reign with Christ, his healing is useless.

All some people do is to come and sleep in the church after sleeping at home. Some come and do not even concentrate on what is going on at all. That which the Lord takes seriously as to allow His own Son to cry in agony on the cross, is regarded as a play thing by some people. All these signs are

Be Prepared

Pointing to the fact that everything is coming to an end. All the things that are happening in the world today, point to the fact that the final subject in the timetable of God is coming up and the last bell can ring at any time. What we are expecting now is the sound of the trumpet.

When the trumpet sounds, the dead in Christ shall be raised, and the living saints too shall at the coming of Christ, be caught up in the air with the Lord. So, both those that have slept in the Lord and those that are still alive would have a common meeting point, when the Lord shall come. That is what we are all waiting for. Anyone that cannot be found at that meeting has wasted his or her time coming to Church, because that is when the roll would be called. Just like that song writer says, "While the roll is called up yonder, I would be there." "When the saints go marching in, Lord, I want to be in that number." That is the number we are talking about. Once a person is not in that number, it would have been better if the person was not born.

Beloved, after the children of God have been withdrawn, what the Bible calls the great tribulation would begin. The great tribulation is better read and imagined than witnessed. I pray that the Lord will help you, in Jesus name.

The Bible says that the tribulation would be so great that men would want to die, but death would be far from them. During this period, great trouble would visit the earth.

After the great tribulation, the saints and the Lord Jesus Christ would come back to the earth and would stay here for one thousand years. Then, the new heaven and the new earth would come and we would forever be with the Lord. So, the next thing in God's programme now is the rapture. God has shown us the example of rapture before at the time of Noah. Only eight people were saved during the flood that took place during the time of Noah. We will dwell more on rapture and the great tribulation in chapters 5 and 6.

Do not allow anyone to deceive you. The final item on God's timetable would take place soon. But before that happens God would withdraw His people from the earth first, before pouring out His undiluted wrath upon the rest. People are saying there is no peace now, the much needed peace would be unavailable at the time of the great tribulation. It would be terrible because the Holy Spirit and the saints of God who had been praying day and night would have been withdrawn. It is as a result of this, that there is this admonition in Matthew 24: 44, which says, *"Therefore, be ye also ready:*

Be Prepared

for in such an hour as ye think not, the Son of man cometh."

If you know you are not yet ready for the coming of the Lord, you better get ready now. God has given His own people an assurance of a prepared place.

"Let not your heart be troubled: ye believe in God, believe also in me. In my Father's house are many mansions: if it were not so, I would have told you. I go to prepare a place for you. And if I go and prepare a place for you, I will come again, and receive you unto myself; that where I am, there ye may be also." (John 14:1-3)

Jesus will come back. I am confident of this because He said so Himself. I want to ask you a question at this point. Do you really believe that Jesus is coming back? If you do, then, it should change your life. You should change from the way you are living now. The Bible says that those who have this hope in them will purify themselves. That is why every child of God must read the story of the transfiguration. Mark 9 : 1- 8 says,

"And he said unto them, verily I say unto you, that there be some of them that stand here, which shall not taste of death, till they have seen the kingdom of God come with power. And after six

six days, Jesus taketh with him Peter, and James,-and John, and leadeth them up into an high mountain apart by themselves: and he was transfigured before them. And his raiment became shinning, exceeding white as snow; so as no fuller on earth can white them. And there appeared unto them Elias with Moses: and they were talking with Jesus. And Peter answered and said to Jesus, Master, it is good for us to be here: and let us make three tabernacles; one for thee, one for Moses and one for Elias. For he wist not what to say, for they were so afraid; And there was a cloud that overshadowed them: and a voice came out of the cloud, saying, This is my he loved Son: hear him. And suddenly, when they had looked round about, they saw no man any more, save Jesus only with themselves'

So, Peter, James and John witnessed the coming of the Kingdom of God in power on the mount of transfiguration. Moses died and went to heaven several years before Jesus came. Elijah did not die, he was just taken up to heaven. So, Moses and Elijah represent two sets of people that will be raptured. Moses represents those who died in the Lord, while Elijah represents those who will be raptured alive. Jesus will be the magnet to magnetize them to heaven. That was why He boldly declared that He is the resurrection and the life. Many people are loyal to their bosses, societies and all kinds of things, but are not loyal to God.

Be Prepared

Some believe that the gospel is for entertainment and as such, all kinds of songs are brought into the gospel. Some men of God are even more interested in worldly shows and entertainment.

All the prophecies in the Bible must come to pass whether you believe it or not. No prophecy of the Bible has ever filed. When God told Sarah that she would bear a son, and the son would multiply throughout the whole earth, it happened. We know that the garden of Eden actually existed. Scientists no longer argue the fact that there was a great flood during the rime of Noah. If the birth of Jesus Christ was a prophecy and it happened, we therefore cannot push the prophecy concerning the rapture aside.

A particular woman of Jerusalem was crying after Jesus as He was being taken to the cross to be crucified. But the response of Jesus surprised all including the woman. Jesus said, "Weep not for me, weep for yourself and your children." Jesus even had to say another worrisome thing; "Woe unto those that are with child in those days." He told them that Jerusalem would be destroyed. Up until now, a part of Jerusalem is still in trouble. When Jesus pointed to the temple at Jerusalem, and said, "Behold, the day is coming when there shall not be one stone upon another that would not be thrown down," they did not believe Him. The stones have not only been thrown down, but a mosque has taken the place of that church now. So, whether you believe it or hot, no prophecy in the word of God has ever failed and will ever fail.

The day of the Lord is coming and we must abandon the stubbornness in our spirits and the pride of our hearts before we can make it. I want you to think about this very well at this moment. All the prophecies concerning the end of the world, even in our country here, have all come to pass before our eyes and people do not take heed of them. The Bible told us that false christs shall arise. Hence, we have had Jesus of Agege, Jesus of Oyingbo and Jesus of Ikot-Ekpene. But where are they now? They are all dead.

Strange news fills the whole world today. It is therefore not strange to read in the pages of newspapers, stories of a father putting his daughter in the family way. A lot of men now impregnate their housemaids, yet, they are not bothered at all about the abomination. All these things are happening just to confirm the prophecies of the Bible. The Bible says, "Iniquities shall abound and the love of many shall wax cold." The Bible also tells us about rumours of wars. War is now an everyday thing in many countries of the world. The time to put an end to the affairs of this wicked world is indeed at hand.

In Revelation 9:6, the Bible tells us an interesting thing that calls for serious meditation. It says, "And in those days men shall desire to die, and death shall flee from them." It would be that serious. God's children are now dressing exactly like the children of the world. They do all kinds of strange things which do not help the cross of Christ at all. Many pastors and brothers are now going about with jerry curled hair.

Against all expectations, many men are now putting on ear rings, yet they claim to be born again. In many places now, it is quite difficult to differentiate between a church congregation and a disco crowd. Many women pastors now dress exactly like Jezebel of the Bible. Many men of faith even resort to all kinds of methods to raise money. It is becoming almost impossible now for believers to dress modestly.

Christians can no longer find their tears when they commit sin. Many preachers are even arranging abortions for their daughters. All kinds of things are happening now, but the time is almost here, when the trumpet shall sound and the Lord will be requiring many things from us. Christians that are presently alive will need more than they already have now to make the rapture. You must put on the whole armour of God right now, you must be filled with the Holy Ghost and you must keep yourself busy for the Lord. An idle hand is a too for the devil. Christ is coming and you must be ready for Him.

Are you ready for that coming? Are you now occupying for the Lord? The answers you give will determine whether or not you are ready. Please pray the following prayer points aggressively.

PRAYER POINTS
1. He that said I should die by the sword, should die by the sword, in the name of Jesus.
2. I turn the weapons of the enemy against the enemy at every moment of my life, in the name of Jesus.
3. I claim perfect health for myself, in the name of Jesus.
4. Let the blood of Jesus cover me, my family and everything that has to do with me, in the name of Jesus.

5. Father Lord, catapult me to spiritual greatness, in the name of Jesus.
6. Everything in my life that the enemy has called impossible, Lord, make them possible, in Jesus name.
7. Every strategy of the enemy against me in my dreams, I command you to be frustrated, in Jesus' name.

Chapter 4

Short Bed and Narrow Blanket

'For the bed is shorter than that a man can stretch himself on it and the covering narrower than that he can wrap himself in it. For the Lord shall rise up as in Mount Perazim, He shall be wroth as in the valley of Gibeon, that He may do His work, His strange work and begin to pass His act, His strange act.'" (Isaiah 28: 20 -21)

Can you imagine a six feet tall man trying to sleep on a short and slim bench of about four feet. He would not be comfortable at all, or a 7 year old boy who wants to use his mother's scarf as covering cloth, the scarf will not cover much of his body. Some parts of his body will be exposed. In these end times, every believer ought to be reading the book of Revelation. If you have not sat down to read the book of Revelation, please try and read it through.

It is the timetable of God concerning our age. It is an important book and can be called the grand-finale of everything. Many people do not read it because they regard it as obscure and unclear. Whereas the book reveals and unveils a lot of things to us. God will not write what He does not want us to understand. If you do not study this book, you will miss out on a lot of information. Without this book, the scripture will not be complete.

The book of Revelation provides answers to a lot of questions about Christian life. It answers such questions as: Will sin continue? Will sorrow, death and pain go on? Where exactly are we in God's plans? When will the church be raptured? Is Christ coming to reign again physically in the world? What are we expecting before Christ comes again? What does 666, the mark of the antichrist mean? Will the world come to an end? Will the present heaven and earth exist forever? Are the saints to spend eternity in heaven or on earth? The answers to all these questions can be found in the book of Revelation.

Many spectacular things have happened in this world, but nothing is going to be as spectacular as what you find in Revelation 1:7 when it begins to happen. Please note that no prophecy of the Bible has ever changed or failed. The passage says: *"Behold, he cometh with clouds and every eye shall see him and they also which pierced him. All kindred of the earth shall wail because of him. Even so, Amen."* Nothing will match this verse when it begins to happen.

God has shown many believers the vision of the second coming of Christ. These revelations make us to understand that a time is coming when all that will count is what one has done for the Lord Jesus Christ. It is then that people will understand the scriptures which say that, "Vanity upon vanity, all is vanity." (Eccl. 12:8) People will then understand that everything else that man is doing is vanity. It will be clear that all those who have been running after the world, have ran after vanity and left the reality.

It is very strange that many present day believers pay much more attention to their bodies than their spirits. These people feed their bodies with the best foods, wear the best clothes, and take care of their bodies in so many other ways, but neglect and starve their spirits which will last for ever. It is of no use to do so much to the body and neglect the spirit. The Bible says, "Dust thou art and unto dust thou shall return." The flesh is not going to heaven, so, it is not interested in salvation.

Be Prepared

That is why it pulls people' back from attending to their spirits.

There are many signs in the Bible that are about to come to pass like the passage we read in Revelation. As a matter of fact, practically all the prophets in the Bible talked about the second coming of Jesus Christ. The first prophet in the Bible was Enoch. The Bible says that Enoch walked with God and he was not, because God took him. Enoch prophesied about the second coming of Christ. Even at that early time of Genesis. Other prophets like Jacob, Balaam, Zechariah, Jeremiah, Isaiah, Daniel, Joel, Amos, Micah, etc, all talked about the second coming of Jesus Christ. Jesus Himself said it so many times in the New Testament. When Jesus went to heaven physically, and the disciples were bothered, the Bible tells us that some angels said to them, "Men of Galilee, why are you gazing at the sky? This same Jesus that has been taken away from you, will come back in like manner, as you have seen him going." Those that pierced Him will cry on that day.

Some believers claim that they were not physically there when Jesus was crucified and pierced. So, they easily absolve themselves from this prophecy. Piercing Jesus, by this scripture, is not a physical act any longer, it is a spiritual thing. The Bible says that after someone has known the way of salvation, tasted of the power of the world to come, received the baptism of the Holy Spirit, came to Church and listened to messages and the person falls away again, such a person is nailing Jesus to the cross the second time.

All the signs pointing to the second coming of Jesus abound all around us. They include the increase of false christs, wars and rumours of war, famine and pestilence. Hatred is filling the earth, and iniquity is abounding in the church. The love of many for God is waxing cold and the gospel is being preached everywhere in the world. The signs of the days of Noah which were merriment and pleasures. are now a common thing. Violence has filled the whole world. People have become lovers of themselves; covetous, boastful, proud, blasphemous and disobedient. They have the form of godliness but deny the power of God.

The Bible says that there will be increased satanic activities, satanic worship and all sorts of negative things to tell us that the end is very close. Sometime ago, someone came to me in the church with some charm hidden in his pocket. As he was talking to me, he was shaking it, hoping to harm me with it.

Be Prepared

This is an example of increased satanic activities. I felt sorry for him. If I had wanted to deal with him the Elijah way, I would have commanded all the charms in his pocket to turn against him. People will hear the word of God very many times, but they will still commit their sins. A time is coming when the bed will be too short, the blanket will be too narrow, and secrets will be known.

The present church is in a sorry state. Many times, we are called sons of God instead of soldiers. When one declares that he is a soldier of Christ, it means that he has laid down his life, and is ready to die for Christ. Nobody joins the armed forces with a promise or feeling that he won't die. The Bible says, "No man who warreth, entangleth himself with the affairs of this world; that he may please him who has appointed him as a soldier." Many people of the present generation unfortunately have never really seen any revival and if we are not careful, we might not experience any before we go. This is because of the way we are living our lives in this present day; allowing the world to mould us. One day, everybody will stand before Jehovah's throne. That day, the bed will be too short and the blanket too narrow and the secrets of all hearts shall be revealed. Some people say, "It's my life and I want to live it my own way." The question is, is it actually your own life? If God wants to withdraw it, you have no power to withhold it.

The greatest miracle one can receive is the salvation of one's soul. If you fail to get saved, all other miracles are worthless and meaningless. I am aware that a lot of people go to church for miracles, but I implore them to get the first miracle, which is the miracle of salvation. Anything in your life that will not make you ready for heaven, or that will make you to be shaking before Jehovah's throne will also prevent you from receiving your miracles from God.

A lot of people have abandoned what God has for them. They are looking after their own things, running after business, contracts, etc, while abandoning the main thing that God has given them to do. Sometime ago, somebody gave me a cassette in which a brother who was said to be dead for six days and later came back to life, said so many things about his experience. He said something which I will never forget. He said that he got to a particular place and they brought out what they called the "Record of Service" and this record was so detailed that he was surprised. It had details like, lateness to church, with two columns on faithfulness and disobedience. The next one was on offering, evangelism, etc.

Everything was neatly planned. He said that when it got to his turn and he looked at the book, he saw that in the area of tithes, faithful was marked for him, but for offering, disobedient was marked for him. When he enquired why disobedient was recorded for him in offering, he was taken through what he did while he was alive. He became worried. Anyway, he came back to life because God said he should go and warn others.

From the book of Isaiah, it is clear that it is alien for God to judge people even though the Bible tells us that God will start His judgement in His house. The passage says, "God will arise and do His strange work and carry out His strange act." This shows that it is not something that God wants to do, but He has to do it. So, if you are reading this message and you know that your life is not secured in the Lord Jesus Christ, or you are playing with sin or with your salvation, you better repent and change now. Today may be the only day that you have to do so. After now, anything can happen to you. There is no point in continuing to live when you are not sure if your life is secured in the Lord Jesus Christ.

Our main passage which is Revelation 20: 11 - 15 says, "And I saw a great white throne, and him that sat on it, from whose face the earth and the heaven fled away and there was found *no place for them. And I saw the dead, small and great, stand before God and the books were opened, and another book was opened which is the book of life, and the dead were judged out of those things which were written in the books, according to their works. And the sea gave up the dead which were in it, and death and hell delivered up the dead which were in them, and they were judged everyone according to their works. And death and hell were cast into the lake of fire. This is the second death. And whosoever was not found written in the book of life was cast into the lake of fire."*

Whosoever here, refers to everybody irrespective of position or status; Pastors, Sunday school teachers, Evangelists, Presidents, Directors general, Engineers, Doctors, etc. As long as the person's name is not found in the book of life, the person will be cast into the lake of fire. This is the stand of God. God lifts up His curtain and makes it possible for people to see the white throne. God will be the judge. The judges of the world may make mistakes, but God will not make mistakes. There are many things we do not know and that are not clear to us now about what will happen at the end of the world. But one thing is certain, we know the Judge, and He cannot make mistakes. A worldly lawyer or judge could be bribed to get a favourable judgement, but this is not possible with God.

The purpose of the judgement is to ensure that God gives due punishment to everyone for the evil deeds they have done.

Now that you are still alive, God is giving you a trial before your condemnation. He is giving you ample chance to decide and prove whether you want to go to heaven or not. The purpose of God's judgement is to judge the secrets of men. To judge all the idle words that we speak, the thoughts, words, actions and sins of men.

God has His own methods of administering judgement. For those who did not hear the gospel before they died, God will judge them according to their conscience. Conscience is God's policeman and there is no one without a conscience. For those who got the law of Moses, followed the law and were able to fulfill the law, they will go to heaven, but those that lived then and failed by the law, will go to hell fire. If you are exposed to the gospel like many of us are now, and refuse to hear and do accordingly, you shall also be judged accordingly.

Behold, the day of judgement is approaching, when the bed will be too short and the blanket will be too narrow. It is necessary that we pray that this day does not meet us unawares. God gave us the Bible because of this. It is now man's time to prove that he will go to heaven. The church is becoming worldly. All kinds of things are happening in the house of God. For example, a man of God was caught committing fornication with a church member. The same church now gave him a rousing send forth after he had been dismissed. This tells us that things that should not be found in the church have entered therein. A lot of preachers are confused because many of their church members are wedded to sin. Whether you believe it or not, judgement will come anyway.

God will sit on His throne and the Bible says the anger in His face will be so much that heaven and earth will flee away, from His sight and presence. All those who are dead from the time of Adam, all over the world will show up, unbelievers will show up too, backsliders, rebellious school children, those who say they have no time for the gospel now, children who have reached the age of accountability, will all be at the judgement seat of God. All those who want to wait to achieve material success before worshipping God seriously will have themselves to blame, because they may never have the opportunity. Now is the time to prove to God that you are

Worthy of heaven.

There is no second chance at judgement and there is no room for repentance. If a sinner remembers the name of Jesus on that day, the name will only torture him. Praying will be too late and excuses, no matter how genuine and true they are, will not be acceptable. I will like to advise you now. If you are struggling with an unbeliever over anything, drop the thing and let the unbeliever have it. This is because there is no time and if God calls at anytime and you are not able to give a proper account of yourself, all your church attendance will be in vain. There will be a great roll call, and those who call themselves nominal Christians, attend beauty contests, watch TV as if TV is the Bible and husbands who run after their house helps at night, will all be present at the judgement seat of God where their secrets shall be revealed.

The judgement seat shall have no class. The high and low shall be merged together. A day is coming said the Lord, when the secret of all earth shall be revealed.

One day, after delivering my message in a church, I noticed that somebody was making noise outside, threatening to beat up another person. People gathered and were begging her to calm down and not to beat the person. It took me some time to realise that I was the one she wanted to beat up. Why? She told the people that somebody must have told me her secrets and that I used her to preach. So, I started to beg her not to beat me up. This same person unfortunately is dead now. That thing which the Lord was telling her to repent from on that day, eventually killed her. When you die, you appear in another world.

The Bible says, "It is given unto man to die once, after that, judgement." Every hidden atrocity, cleverly concealed sins and hidden lusts will be exposed on that day. All the people who are spiritual "submarines" will be known. Some people come to church and behave as if they are serving the pastor. Some try to physically avoid the men of God because they know their activities are unclean. They keep immoral books at home and carry the Bible to church to camouflage. If you are this type of person, you are a hypocrite and you are doing yourself a lot of harm. All these will be revealed on that day. The parable of the dog going back to its vomit will then apply to you. You should not be interested in the honour of man or earthly posts. You should be interested in God's honour and seek after it diligently.

A lot of people who come to church are not interested in

personal spiritual growth. In spite of the messages they listen to, they still do not change from their evil ways. They feel sober when in church, but go back to those things that made them to feel bad soon after they leave the church. Whereas the Bible says, "Shall we continue in sin that grace may abound? God forbid." Miracles cannot multiply when we remain in sin. The devil keeps running after people because they possess his property. You have to repent. If you are to stand now before the judgement seat of Christ, what will you say?

There are only two ways; the broad way and the narrow way. There is no center. The broad way leads to hell and the narrow way leads to glory. There are only two types of people: the saved sinners and the unsaved sinners. The Bible calls them the sheep' and the goat or the living and the dead. There are only two deaths, the death of the righteous and the death of the wicked. There are only two futures, the kingdom of heaven and hell fire.

These days, a lot of people want to copy the fashion of the world which the Bible describes as "fading away." The devil has taken hold of the literature world and is using all the funny pornographic magazines to confuse people. Parents should be careful of the type of materials that circulate in their homes so that God will not judge them for confusing their children. Anything not good for the youths, is not good for the adults. It is a shame on our society that the best selling magazines and materials are the immoral ones.

Many churches are beautiful outwardly but inside, they contain the bones of dead men. God is tired of lip service. He wants heart service. God will not respect bench warmers but only true worshipers. Do not be like the proverbial frog that wanted to fly on borrowed wings, he hit a rock and fell down. Do not live your life on borrowed spiritual wings. Your faith cannot rely on someone else's. You have to develop yourself personally. Your relationship with God must be personal.

DESTRUCTIVE TRINITIES

Money, alcohol and sex are what is known as the trinity of spiritual failure. If any of these things is in your life, then you are on a direct express way to hell fire. There is also the trinity of defeat comprising doubt, worry and fear. If you entertain any of these, you are going to hell. The master of these trinities is the trinity of destruction which comprises sin, death and hell. If you love yourself, you must hate all these trinities to avoid going to hell fire.

Be Prepared

There is no accident on the way to hell because the way is broad and wide. The good news is that God has not made provision for anyone to perish, so the decision to perish is personal. On the day of judgement, the bed will be too short and the blanket will be too narrow and nothing shall be covered. Every evil deed will be exposed.

Some people have the call of God on their lives but they are joking and playing with it. Some of us are seeking recognition that God does not want us to seek. A lot of people carry fake smiles on their faces even when they are not happy. On that day, the bed will be too short and the blanket will be too narrow. If you have any sin to confess, confess it to the Holy Spirit now. Repent and beg for forgiveness. You can also deceive yourself if you want to, by pretending that you have no sin. Please readjust your life and rededicate yourself to God.

PRAYER POINTS
1. I rebuke the spirit of backsliding, in Jesus name.
2. Father Lord, anything that will remove me from your presence, take it away from me, in the name of Jesus.
3. Fire of God, purge away every filthiness from my spirit, in the name of Jesus.

Be Prepared

4. Father Lord, give me power to subdue the flesh, in the name of Jesus.
5. Oh Lord, give me the grace to focus on the Lord Jesus all the time, in the name of Jesus.
6. Father Lord, help me to be heavenly minded all the days of my life, in the name of Jesus.
7. Oh Lord, give me the grace to love you and cling unto you, in the name of Jesus.
8. I withdraw myself from the camp of the enemies, in the name of Jesus.
9. Let the word of God prosper in my life, in the name of Jesus.

Chapter 5

The Rapture

Beloved, this message focuses on the greatest event that is to happen in the history of mankind. This event is known as the "RAPTURE"

Many years ago, I realized that majority of those who got born again in the olden days were more on fire for God than those that are born again now. Those who were brought up under the old-fashion Christianity were always very hot for God. It took a few of them then to move mountains for God. But the present day Christians do not take the things of God seriously. You find some so-called Christians with their legs crossed and throwing peanuts into their mouths while listening to the word of God on the Television. These kinds of Christians are known as "Church grasshoppers". The present day Christians waste a lot of God's useful time doing

Irrelevant things in the house of God e.g. committee meetings and unnecessary ceremonies.

In those days, the method of their preaching gave rise to hot Christians. What do I mean by that? There was no day you came to church, that you would not be told that sin is bad and unprofitable. You would hear that hell is hot and undesirable, that judgement is absolutely certain and that God will make no mistakes. You would hear that eternity is long, enjoyable, and must not be toyed with. You would also hear that salvation is free and anybody who perished, did so by his own design. The preachers also made it known to people that they needed to make conscious effort not to perish. The prayer meetings then were more serious than what we have now.

In those days, nobody offered anybody any help. There was a programme for those who wanted to receive the baptism of the Holy Spirit called, "TARRY A LITTLE," held on Fridays. Sometimes, at this programme, you find up to two hundred people out of a church of about five hundred people. The coordinator normally came there, sang a little chorus and would say, "Begin to ask for the baptism of the Holy Ghost, in the name of Jesus." Everybody would begin to pray seriously. After a while, he would stop them and say, "You people are not serious, you should pray more aggressively, no matter how you are feeling." Sometimes, nobody laid hands on anybody. There were no lectures.

Occasionally, after the prayer meeting, the coordinator would ask, "How many of you have received the Holy Spirit? Five people out of two hundred would raise up their hands and the others would cry home because they failed to receive. That was the level of enthusiasm and the seriousness for things of God then.

The Bible says; "If the Spirit of Him that raises Christ from the dead is in you, it shall quicken your mortal body." But when the Spirit is not there, nothing will quicken the mortal body. These days, when somebody prays for the baptism of the Holy Spirit and does not receive it, he will go somewhere, take a drink and go home instead of feeling sad and working harder. Then, only five people may receive the Holy Ghost baptism at a meeting, and by the time you see them again, they would be boiling with fire. They would be prophesying and seeing visions. I think we should go back to those methods. You may call the olden days Christians names, but they had fire burning within them.

A lot of people die and go to hell fire everyday. The fact that you are not among them is God's grace and not because you are clever or special. It is because God wants to preserve your life for certain things. It will be a great tragedy if you hold back the hand of God and prevent him from doing what He wants to do with your life. The Bible tells us that when Jesus got to His own town, His hands were tied. He could not do many miracles because of their unbelief. They limited God. It is possible for somebody to abort the programme of God for his life.

WHAT IS THE RAPTURE?
I Thessalonians 4: 13-17 says, *"But I would not have you to be ignorant brethren, concerning them which are asleep, that ye sorrow not, even as others which have no hope. For if we believe that Jesus died and rose again, even so them also which sleep in Jesus will God bring with him. For this we say unto you by the word of the Lord, that we which are alive and remain unto the coming of the Lord shall not prevent them which are asleep. For the LORD himself shall descend from heaven with a shout, with the voice of the archangel, and with the trump of God; and the dead in Christ shall rise first. Then we which are alive and remain shall be caught up together with them in the clouds, to meet the LORD in the air; and so shall we ever be with the LORD."*

Be Prepared

That scripture says that the LORD Himself will descend with the sound of the trumpet, then all those who died in Christ will arise. Then, those of us who are alive and by the grace of God, born-again and living a holy life, shall be caught up to meet them in the air. This catching up of people, both living and dead is what is known as "RAPTURE" John 14:1- 3 says,

"Let not your heart be troubled; ye believe in God, believe so in me. In my Father's house there are many mansions; if it were not so, I would have told you. I go to prepare a place for you. And if I go and prepare a place for you, I will come again and receive you unto myself; that where I am, there ye may be also."

It will be a wonderful time. It will be very unfortunate for someone to come to church, spend his life as a Christian and not get to heaven.

"If we believe that Jesus is coming back, our lives should change. The Bible says that while the disciples of Jesus were busy wondering, and gazing at the sky after Jesus ascended, two men in dazzling white raiment stood by them and said, you men of Galilee, why stand gazing at the sky?

Be Prepared

This same Jesus that is taken away from you, shall come back in like manner which you see him go.

Those who know God do not argue with God's Word. This is the time to gird our loins because there is no sign preceeding the rapture that has not happened, Just as Noah was saved from the flood, the LORD will take His church away before He pours His wrath on the earth, The rapture may occur at any time. A lot of people are loyal to their churches and denominations, but they are not loyal to God. The gospel has become a thing of entertainment in many places nowadays. Some men of God are even more interested in show business than in preaching the Word of God and pastors of Bible-believing churches are having great problems because many born-again Christians do not take heed to obey what they read in the Bible or are taught.

Why will the rapture take place?
1. For Christ to receive the saints to Himself like we read in John 14.
2. To resurrect the dead in Christ (I Corinthians 15:51)
3. To take the saints to heaven.
4. To change the bodies of saints to immortality. These bodies that are suffering from diseases and

afflictions will be changed to immortality.
5. To present the saints before God. Jesus Christ will say, Father, here are the ones you committed to my hands. I bring them back to You.
6. To cause the saints to escape the tribulations, because once the rapture takes place, God will pour out His cup of anger on mankind and peace shall be withdrawn.

Those who are left behind will suffer terrible consequence
For rejecting Jesus.

When will the rapture take place?

The rapture can take place anytime, but only God the Father knows when it will be. Sometime ago, a man died and as some people were washing his body in preparation for burial, he suddenly opened his eyes and said, "Thank you for washing this body. I just want to tell you certain things. Jesus was already on His way back to the earth. But He was asked to wait a little bit. If not He would have come back a few days ago." This means that the Almighty God can release Him now to go and gather His people and He will not listen to excuses.

Be Prepared

How long would the rapture take?
It will happen so fast that unbelievers and fake Christians will be shocked. The Bible says that it will happen in a twinkling of an eye. When rapture happens, our physical bodies would become glorified. We will still be able to touch, talk and recognize one another. Our glorified bodies will be free from ageing, sickness, pain and death, in that glorified body, you can appear and disappear at will, contrary to our mortal bodies which are subject to death and decay. That is why the Bible says, "*But this corruptible body, must put on incorruption, and this mortal body must put on immortality.*" That is when the scripture which says that death is swallowed up in victory will come to pass. If that does not happen in a person's life, it means that death actually succeeded in capturing the person for good.

The question is: Are you troubled by thoughts of the future events? Are you afraid when you think about the return of Christ? Are you aware that no man can stop the return of Christ? Do you know that it does not matter whether you believe it or not? Do you know that those who miss the rapture will face the great tribulation? Are you aware at all that the devil hates you and I, and is interested in killing and sending everyone to hell fire? Are you sure that your name is in the book of life? If for example the trumpet sounds now, and God says, son or daughter, it is enough, come home. Are you confident that you will go to heaven? If you are confident that you will make heaven, you will not be dreaming of masquerades, spirit husbands and wives, eating in the dream, etc. Instead, you will be seeing the LORD Jesus Christ or His holy angels. Your dream world will be another teaching session from the Lord. How dare somebody say, "I am going to reign with Christ," when every night he is busy fighting masquerades. Do you presently attend a church that has no effect on your spiritual life? Do you hate messages on holiness and holy living? If in your church, you are not taught that any sin in your life, no matter how little, would make you miss the rapture, then you are going to the wrong church and you must get out. If you stay put, your story might become like that of Lot. You cannot blame anyone or anything if you miss the rapture.

Qualifications for making the rapture
1. *You must he born again.*

Many people have turned this terminology upside down. To some, being born-again means to wear long shirts, long blouses, tie head scarves and look sad. To some, it means walking and talking very gently. To some, it is becoming exactly like the world, while you talk about Jesus. Being born-again is realizing that you are a sinner and coming unto the LORD to save you from your sins and you repenting completely. Being born-again is not a title, it is an experience. Whosoever is in Christ has become a new creation, old things have passed away, behold all things have become new. Not that old things will be polished or refurbished they must become new.

2. *You must be in Christ.*
It is possible to be in church and not be in Christ. It is possible to be at church but not in Church. People must be able to see you and say, behold, a child of God. Christ must be in you.

3. *You must be holy.*

4. *You must live and walk in the Spirit.*
The Bible says that if you live by the flesh, you shall die.

5. *You must be in God's will for your life.*

6. *You must put on the whole armour of God and not part of the armour.*

7. *You must become as a child.* The Bible says that except you accept the kingdom of God as a child, you cannot enter into it. Childlike faith is of God.

As soon as the rapture happens and the saints have been taken away, there will be no electricity, water and telephone. Nobody will be able to go to work or anywhere because, drivers who are born-again will be gone and there will be all kinds of accidents. Believers who will be driving their cars would be raptured. People carrying coffins to the mortuary or cemeteries would discover all of a sudden that the corpses have disappeared from their hands. Prisoners will vanish from their prisons. The hospitals will be filled with accident victims. Businesses will close down. There will be chaos everywhere. Those left behind will be confused. They will not understand what happened, because it will be sudden. This is why one has to pray and be ready.

Churches will be packed full, because everybody will rush there on that day in a bid to find out what happened. Preachers who will miss the rapture will be made miserable by members of their churches who missed it too. They will ask them why they did not tell them the truth. They will ask them why they failed to tell them that they needed to work harder than they did to make heaven. And the preachers will say, "Leave us alone, you all went to school and you have your Bibles."

Beloved, we must recognize the fact that Jesus did not die so that pastors will be collecting salaries. He came for a much more serious purpose. People will be ready to mob pastors who are afraid now to tell their members the truth so that they will not run away. On that day, marriage ceremonies will become chaotic, because some bridegrooms and brides will disappear in the middle of the programme. Genuine Christians will be missing and all those who insist on drinking alcohol and being fashionable will be left behind.

The Bible tells us that there are some people in heaven, hurrying God up, saying "How long, oh Lord of Host will you watch these people do what they are doing? Please, avenge our blood on their heads." Aborted babies will be crying, "O Lord, how long will you allow these women who aborted us to continue in their sin?"

Isaac Newton the clever and popular scientist who was a Christian told a man about the rapture and the man began to argue with him. After the man had listened to the messages on the rapture and the second coming of the Lord, he laughed and said to Isaac Newton, "Supposing somebody dies and his body is divided into several pieces. One leg is eaten by a lion, the second one is thrown into the river and the other parts of the body burnt to ashes and the ashes sprinkled all over many countries, when the rapture happens, how will the man be gathered together again? Isaac, Newton took sand, sawdust and little pieces of iron and mixed them together. After he mixed everything together, he asked the man, "Is it possible to get these pieces of iron out of this mixture? The man said, "Impossible." Then Isaac Newton took a magnet and ran it through the mixture and all the pieces of iron stuck to the magnet. After this experiment, he said to the man, "If God can give this power to an ordinary stone, how much more the Rock of ages who has all the powers. A songwriter says,

> Lord, I care not for riches,
> neither silver nor gold,
> I would make sure of heaven,
> I would enter the fold.
> In the book of Thy kingdom
> with its pages so fair,
> Tell me, Jesus, my Saviour
> is my name written there?

Many years ago, a man surrounded his poultry with barbed

wires. One day, a lean and hunger-stricken fox entered the poultry through a small hole by the barbed wire. It started feeding on chicken and became very fat. One day, the owner of the poultry noticed that his chicken were disappearing and said that he would kill whatsoever was stealing them. As he was talking, the fox heard and decided to escape when the man left. He tried to run out through the way he came in, but unfortunately it had become too fat for the hole. It did not have any choice but to start fasting. After a week, it went back to the hole and was able to get out.

The above illustration explains what the world is like. We brought nothing into the world and we will take nothing out of it. Everything we acquire here, will be lost here. If you attend the Mountain of Fire and Miracle Ministries and does not succeed in getting to heaven, it will be a terrible waste. I thank God for every miracle you receive here, but the final victory is when we all appear before the LORD Jesus Christ and He says, "Welcome, thou good servant, enter into the joy of Your master."

Beloved, where will you end up? Those things that believers used to run away from in the past, are what present-day Christians are playing with. Examine your life to know whether you are qualified to go with the lord if the trumpet sounds now.

PRAYER POINTS

1. Pray against the spirit of backsliding and lukewarmness.

2. You the spirit of procrastination, I bind you, in the name of Jesus.

3. O Lord, deliver me from spiritual coldness, in the name of Jesus.

4. I remove my name from every evil record, in the name of Jesus.

5. I refuse to follow the programme of the devil for my life, in the name of Jesus.

Chapter Six

The Coming Great Event

I would like you to open your mind as you read this chapter. This topic is not what many people like to talk about. Nonetheless, it is one of the greatest truths in the word of God. It is about the end of the world, the second coming of Christ, the rapturing of the saints, and indeed, the judgement of God. This message, therefore, discusses the events of which no man can do anything about, just as no man can stop the sun from shining, and the morning from coming into being.

It is really not important whether you believe it or not. What is important is that the word of God says it is true, and the word of God is more than the word of any man. Everything that is happening now is pointing to the fact that this great event is around the corner. It is unfortunate that most people are not seeing it. The Bible tells us categorically that there is a time when great trouble would come upon the world and the Bible calls that period, "The great tribulation." The prophecies concerning this great event are already happening. Most of the prophecies are becoming history and many people are still shying away from the truth.

Sometime ago, the Lord showed me a vision of the tribulation. I saw in the vision that the Lord came, and many things beyond description happened. Although some people were raptured with Him, numberless others just disappeared like that Immediately the vision cleared off, I heard from the Lord "that" what I saw was the great tribulation. What I saw worried me. I saw many dead bodies on the street and people trampled on them but they did not bother about them.

The Lord told me that during the tribulation period, life would become meaningless as peace would be removed. It is because there is peace now, that is why people can move around the way they want. The Bible has a terrible picture of what would happen. So, it does not matter whether you believe it or not. One thing is sure, everything the Bible has prophesied about this period has happened to the last letter. I can assure you that if you do not believe that the great tribulation would come, then you do not believe in the second coming of Jesus Christ.

If you do not have God as your Lord, another god will replace Him in your life. You can never be spiritually neutral. You are either for God or for the devil. There is nothing like being a free thinker. All free thinkers are thinking for the devil. What you should be waiting for now should be the same as the earnest expectation of all believers, as it is written in I Thessalonians 4:13-18:

"But I would not have you to be ignorant, brethren, concerning them which are asleep, that ye sorrow not, even as others which have no hope. For if we believe that Jesus died and rose again, even so them also which sleep in Jesus will God bring with him. For this we say unto you by the word of the Lord that we which are alive and remain unto the coming of the Lord shall not prevent them which are asleep. For the Lord himself shall descend from heaven with a shout, with the voice of the archangel, and with the trump of God and the dead in Christ shall rise first. Then we which are alive and remain shall be caught up together with them in the clouds to meet the Lord in the air and so shall we ever be with the Lord. Wherefore comfort one another with these words."

So this is what we are all waiting for now and it can happen at anytime. It may happen when we are sleeping or while we are awake. It can happen at anytime. The Bible repeats the same thing in I Corinthian 15:51-52:

"Behold, I shew you a mystery; We shall not all asleep, but we shall all be changed. In a moment, in the twinkling of an eye, at the last trump for the trumpet shall sound, and the dead shall be raised incorruptible, and we shall be changed."

The Lord is coming with His trumpet. It will be too sad if a believer fails to hear that trumpet. The Bible divides the whole of Gods programme into seven and gives each programme one thousand years. The last one thousand years is what is before us. The Bible is quite emphatic when it says, six days shall thou labour. The six thousandth year of that labour is about to end and the Lord is coming to receive His saints unto Himself. He says,

"Let not your heart be troubled, believe in God and believe in me, also, for in my Father's house there are many mansions. If it were not so, I would have told you. I am going to prepare a place, when I prepare that place I will come and take you to my Father, so that where I am, you may be there also." (John 14:1-3)

Jesus is indeed coming to receive His own to Himself. He is coming to resurrect the dead in Christ. He is coming to take the saints to heaven where they will receive their reward and where they will partake of the marriage supper of the Lamb. He is coming to change the body to an immortal one. He is coming to present the saints to His Father. He is coming to remove the author of lawlessness. He is coming to permit the revelation of the Antichrist, and He is coming to enable the saints to escape the great tribulation.

Please open your mind to this message. Once that trumpet sounds, you will not be able to change your camp. Maybe you are still sitting in your dead church or where there is no God at all. Maybe, you are serving God and you are still living in sins, and evil thoughts occupy your heart daily. May be you are still dreaming of witchcraft spirits and masquerades. May be you cannot remove yourself from the clutch of evil forces. You are still keeping malice and getting angry at people all time.

Maybe you are just coming to church and you are not a serious Christian. Maybe God does not speak to you, and you have never seen any vision in your life, nor know the voice of God when He is speaking. Maybe you are still committing sins in secret and you are covering them from the sight of men. Maybe you are still unfaithful to your husband or to your wife. I wish to make it clear to you that once you are living an unserious life as listed above, and the trumpet sounds, you certainly cannot be raptured with Christ.

No word can describe adequately the woes of the victims of the great tribulation. Tribulation comes from the word 'Tribolium' It is interpreted to mean a threshing hammer. The, Bible calls it the time of "Jacob's trouble." Jews have suffered a lot. Hiltler killed six million of them, but God says, there is more punishment coming for them, especially during the tribulation period.

You may ask the question; "Why should God allow people to pass through the tribulation?" The answer is simple. It is punishment for neglecting Christ, for the unrepentant Jews, and judgement upon the world for refusing to hear the call of the gospel. So, it would be a time of terrible trouble. It is better for us to read about it than to experience it. You should prayerfully read it in the Bible and make yourself ready to be raptured with Christ once the trumpet sounds.

Make up your mind now not to be a partaker in the tribulation that will happen on earth hereafter. Various

prophets gave the great tribulation names.
Daniel 12: 1 says, *"And at that time shall Michael stand up, the great prince which standeth for the children of thy people: and there shall be a time of trouble, such as never was since there was a nation even to that same time..."*

Daniel clarified the time as that 91 great trouble. Jeremiah 30:7 says;

" Alas! For that day is great, so that none is like it: it is even the time of Jacob's trouble; but he shall be saved out of it."

Isaiah 24:17-21 recorded the following fearful verses:
"Fear, and the pit, and the snare are upon thee, O inhabitant of the earth. And it shall come to pass, that he who fleeth from the noise of the fear shall fall into the pit and he that cometh up out of the midst of the pit shall be taken in the snare for the windows from on high are open, and the foundations of the earth do shake. The earth is utterly broken down, the earth is clean dissolved, the earth is moved exceedingly. The earth shall reel to and fro like a drunkard, and shall be removed like a cottage and the transgression thereof shall be heavy upon it; and it shall fall, and not rise again. And it shall come to pass

in that day that the Lord shall punish the host of the high ones that are on high, and the kings of the earth upon the earth."

If the Old Testament prophets said so much about the great tribulation, no one should be in doubt. It would be a terrible day.

Beloved, this message concerns a believer who does not want to miss the rapture. It is that time that people will find out that their certificates are useless. Judgement will be based on one's stewardship and what one has done or did not do for the Lord Jesus Christ. Those who are in the secret societies will then see on that day, that a great punishment awaits them. The punishment will also affect those who are hiding all types of things underneath their beds, and are mixing their Christianity with all kinds of satanic junks.

Matthew 24 : 21 says, "For then shall be great tribulation, such as was not since the beginning of the world to this time, no, nor ever shall be. "That means that, that type of tribulation has never been before. The Bible says it will not be seen again. It is great mystery that many have not seen the handwriting on the wall. When you want to observe God's time-table, and you really want to know how God is operating, the nation to look at is the nation of Israel. God raised them up, for a particular purpose and so many foes have attacked them, but they have not succeeded.

In 1948, they fought a war, the Arabs outnumbered them with a ratio of about 40 to 1. The war lasted for about seven months, but Israel won. There was another one in about 1956, Israel won again. There, was yet another war in 1967, that was when, they got Jerusalem back, they won. There was another one in 1973 which they also won. These are the fulfillment of God's prophecy. What God has been saying in the Bible is becoming history now, and many people are not observing it.

There would be a time of great tribulation. Immediately the saints are taken away, then hell will be let loose upon the whole world. The saints are the people who have the Holy Spirit. They are the ones praying and interceding. When you remove the intercessor, or remove those people calling on the Lord our God, hell will be let loose. A man will now take control of the whole world. He would take up the name of the antichrist. Although he has not yet manifested physically for us to see, nevertheless, he has manifested in many lives. As Christ was an incarnation of holiness, the

Antichrist will be an incarnation of sin. As Christ was filled with the Holy Spirit, the antichrist will be filled with unclean spirits.

As Christ had love, humility, mercy, and patience, the antichrist will be filled with abomination, wickedness and hypocrisy. Christ received His power from above, the antichrist will receive his from below. Christ was here to minister to man for three and half years. The antichrist shall give the unraptured people hell for three and half years. As Christ humble Himself, the antichrist shall break the law.

Christ made Himself poor so that you may be rich, the antichrist will make himself rich. Christ was hated when He was in the world but men will love the antichrist. Christ brought peace into the world, the antichrist will bring organized confusion. As Christ came to do the will of God, the antichrist shall come to do the will of the devil. As Christ is the good shepherd, the antichrist will be the devouring wolf. Just as the Holy Spirit heralded the coming of Christ, demons will also herald the coming of the antichrist. It is already happening now, and is working in the lives of many in the church.

I was once at a wake-keeping ceremony of a late Christian brother. While we were yet singing that he should sleep on in the land where no lights or days were seen, some people suddenly challenged us to stop singing. They said it was time for them to perform their own rituals. After sometime, people began to enter with strange uniforms, they switched off the light and rushed to the man's bedroom. The believers did not wait to be told to disappear before they did. But in the church on Sundays, before he died, he was a dutiful usher. But the role did not shape his Christian life. While he was ushering people into God's kingdom, he had become a sign- post himself. The thing about the sign post is that, it- will never leave where it is. It will only point the way to the place. He was a sign post which ushered people into God's kingdom but in the end, he belonged to satan's kingdom. That is the spirit of the antichrist and it is operating in many lives today, and confusing many people.

A brother also told me about the evil that took place in his former church before every service. He said that they would prepare incense and then drop a bit of marijuana (hemp) into it. When the people sniffed it, there would be confusion and they would say that the Spirit of God was moving. But it was rather the spirit of the antichrist.

Any spirit that will throw anyone on the ground and make

him or her to disorganize the benches is not the Holy Spirit. It is the spirit of the antichrist. The Holy Ghost is as gentle as a dove and He is the comforter. The brother also revealed that whenever they wanted a man to stop loving his wife, they would take a candle, write the name of the wife on it and thereafter perform certain rituals. Antichrist fight in the church! Some so called prophets pray for cocaine pushers. They pray for thieves, so that the course of justice will be perverted whenever they have a case in court and they will pray that innocent people should be jailed.

The spirit of antichrist is greatly at work! It is already in the world. Will you allow it to grab you? When the trumpet sounds, where will you be? Or don't you know that an unraptured believer cannot do anything in the midst of the witches and wizards left behind. Revelation 13 gives an in-depth insight into what will happen on that day. Read this chapter very well and understand it. This world is not a world you should live in anyhow. It is not a world you should be infatuated with. It does not make sense, because it is passing away.

If you refuse to leave the world, the world will leave you. A man of 150 years cannot be looking for prostitutes. People will have to carry him there and the prostitutes will not answer him. So, if you refuse to leave sin, it will leave you and at that time, it would have made you useless.

Revelation 13:1-18 says, "And I stood upon the sand of the sea (The sea there means people) and saw a beast rise up out of the sea, having seven heads and ten horns, and upon his horns ten crowns, and upon his heads the name of blasphemy. And the beast which I saw was like unto a leopard, and his feet were as the feet of a bear, and his mouth as the mouth of a lion and the dragon i.e. (the devil) gave him his power and his seat and great authority."

So, the devil gave the antichrist power and great authority. He offered him his seat and his power.

Verse- 3 says, "And I saw one of his heads as it were wounded to death; and his deadly wound was healed and all the world wondered after the beast." So, the Bible says the people of the world will wonder after the beast. They will confess that the antichrist is wonderful.

Verse 4 -8 says, "And they worshipped the dragon which gave power unto the beast, saying who is like unto the beast? Who is able to make war with him? (People will ask, "Who is able to make war with the antichrist?" He will have lots of military armoury.) "And there was given unto him a mouth speaking great things and blasphemies, and power was given unto him to continue forty and two months. And he opened his mouth in blasphemy against God, to blaspheme his name and his tabernacle, and them that dwell in heaven. And it was given unto him to make war with the saints, and to overcome them and power was given him over all kindred and tongues, and nations. And all that dwell upon the earth shall worship him, whose names are not written in the book of life of the Lamb slain from the foundation of the world."

Verses 12 - 14 says, "And he exerciseth all the power of the first beast before him, and causeth the earth and them which dwell therein to worship the first beast, whose deadly wound was healed. And he doeth great wonders, so that he maketh fire come down from heaven on the earth in the sight of men. And deceiveth them that dwell on the earth, by the means of those miracles which he had power to do in the sight of the beast, saying to them that dwell on the earth, that they should make an image to the beast, which had the wound by a sword, and did live" (He will be doing all kinds of wonders and all that are in the world shall worship him)

Verse 16-18, **"And he causeth all, both small and great, rich and poor, free and bond, to receive a mark in their right hand, or in their foreheads. And that no man might buy or sell, save he that had the mark, or the name of the beast, or the number of his name. Here is wisdom. Let him that hath understanding count the number of the beast; for it is the number of a man; and his number is Six hundred, three score and six (666).**

So, if a person does not receive that mark, the person will not be able to buy or sell anything. It will surprise you that many products now carry the number.

Revelation 14 :11 says, **"And the smoke of their torments ascended up for ever and ever; and they had not rest day nor night, who worship the beast and his image and whosoever receiveth the mark of his name."**

Be rest assured, that anybody who receives this mark is doomed forever. People who do not have the mark will not be able to buy food neither will they be able to go out. But people who receive the mark are forever doomed and hell fire is their place. This is a prophecy of the Bible that must come to pass. Some of the Biblical prophecies have happened and the other ones will happen as well; and that spirit of antichrist is already in operation now. What will you do when you cannot find those you are praying with again? What will you do when you look for the preachers and you cannot find them, particularly those people you considered to be strange, the chronic S.U (Scripture Union) people who refuse to sit down in their homes; who are always preaching. You will discover that day, that they did not just wake up to be preaching about! Maybe you say that you do not carry your own religion on your head, but Jesus carried His own religion on His head. So, why do you want to hide your own Christianity? Did you not read it in the scripture that you cannot light your candle and put it under the bushel? Why do you want to hide your own light and religion?

The spirit of the antichrist is already on the streets. Strange things are happening in the churches now. Many ministers are beginning to take their children to doctors for abortion. We have started having women bishops. The church of orunmila now exits. There are Bazaars all over the place. I saw a van on which somebody wrote "Chrislam." All these things are signs that the spirit of the antichrist is already around. Somebody will be in the house of God and yet his mind will be flying about, thinking about many things e.g. business, television, food, girlfriend, boyfriend, etc. It is the spirit of antichrist that is making all these things to manifest.

business, television, food, girlfriend, boyfriend, etc. It is the spirit of antichrist that is making all these things to manifest.

Once the truth is preached to you and something inside of you rejects it, then something is wrong. Some people come to the church with gum in their mouth. The Bible says that evil men shall wax stronger and stronger and wicked people shall continue in their murder. The Bible reveals many groups of murderers. If you hate your neighbour, according to the Bible, you are a murderer. You don't have to physically kill somebody before you commit murder, once you hate your neighbour, you are a murderer. You are a murderer when you don't have the love of Christ in you.

If you hate your wife, kids, brethren, your father and mother, the Bible calls you a murderer. The Bible says death and life are in the power of the tongue. People who are committing murder with their mouths everyday are murderers according to the standards of the Bible. People who are committing abortions are murderers. All husbands who ask their wives to abort are murderers. Wives too who are committing fornication are murderers. The Bible calls those who kill themselves daily with cigarettes and alcohol murderers. Those who kill themselves with worry, are destroying the temple of God. When you worry about temporal things, the Bible calls you a murderer. There are many people worshipping false gods now. They shall see their reward in due season.

There are various grades of people the Bible calls thieves; they are stealing God's time and money. The message according to the Bible is, watch and pray, so that that day will not come upon you unawares.

Be prepared! Remember that song which says, *"O sinner man, how dare you. You want to stand before God, you want to stand in the judgment unprepared to meet God?* Many people who are coming to church are not Christians at all. I don't want you to be somebody who is just doing false Christianity or playing church because the great tribulation will come, and you must make the rapture. Abandon anything that will disturb you from making the rapture now. You have no excuse whatsoever. Excuses of your husband, wife, children, job, etc., will not be acceptable on the day of great tribulation.

The maximum anyone can live is probably 100 or 200 years. But by the time one gets to that age, one is already useless. However, with eternity, the difference is distinct. Eternity has no end. If you go to the bar-beach and begin to count the sand granules; no matter how long it takes you to do that, it cannot be as long as eternity. Eternity is endless because at that time, the Lord will remove calendars, clocks, etc.

PRAYERS

Talk to the Lord now. Anything at all, no matter how small that can prevent you from being raptured will make you to qualify for the great tribulation. Pray the following prayer point to God now. "Father Lord, examine my life this hour and whatever will prevent me from seeing your face, remove them from my life. I don't want to come to the world in vain, but I want to see your face at the end of the age, in the name of Jesus.

"The Bible says that God is not mocked. You cannot deceive God. You can only deceive yourself. You know the condition of your heart at this moment, and you know that there are certain things you need to confess and ask the lord for forgiveness. Say this, "Lord, I want a transformation in my life now." If you know that there are things you need to sort out with God this hour, lay your hand on your chest and specifically about what you have been doing. Tell the Lord that you have not been spending your time for Him.

If you know you have not given your life to Christ, you have not openly declared your life for Him and you want to take that step this moment. If you don't want the devil to push you to hell fire, and you want to be serious with your Christian life, repeat this confession: "Father, in the name of Jesus, I come before you this moment, I know that the devil is bad and that he doesn't have anything good for me. At this moment Lord, enter into my life in a new way and deliver me from the bondage of sin and the bondage of death. I give my life unto you, in Jesus' name, Father Lord, I pray that you lay your hands on me. As from today, I will no longer be the same. Let your Spirit ignite my spirit and your fire be upon my soul, in the name of Jesus. Bless me abundantly and give me that grace to stand in your presence, in Jesus name."

PRAYER POINTS
1. Spirit of the living God, fall afresh upon me, in Jesus name.
2. Lord, cover me with the blood of Jesus, in Jesus name.
3. I bind every spirit of sudden and premature death, in the name of Jesus.

4. I bind every spirit of death in my household and anyone close to me, in Jesus' name.
5. I bind every blood sucking demon from my ways, in Jesus name.
6. Lord, anywhere that I will put leg and you will not support it, prevent me from going there, in the name of Jesus.
7. Every demonic activity resulting in death, I bind you. I decree that you will not operate in my life, in Jesus name.
8. I bind every spirit of infirmity, in Jesus name.
9. Father Lord, give me the power to live a holy life, in Jesus name.
10. I cleanse my body, soul and spirit from every filthiness with the blood of Jesus, in Jesus name.
11. Father Lord, remove from my life, anything that will prevent me from entering into your kingdom, in Jesus name.

Chapter 7

The White Throne Judgement

Lord, we know that through this message, You will move and your promise that never changes shall come to pass. It is written that every knee shall bow and every tongue shall confess that Jesus is Lord. We know that you will fulfill this promise. Therefore, every contrary knee that is against the Lord Jesus, whether internal or external should bow, in the name of Jesus. Speak unto our hearts and remove our names from the book of prayerlessness. Transport us to the mountain that is higher than us. Thank you Lord Jesus, in Jesus name.

In this chapter, we are looking at an event that we are supposed to know about. Anything that a man does in this world, whether good or bad has a day of reckoning; a day when such; would be made public. It does not matter how carefully such must have been concealed, they would be revealed on that day of judgment and what a shame would it be for the acts that one thought were done in secret to be made public to everybody, that is why it is better for you to depart from your shameful act because the whole universe will soon get to know about it.

Many years ago, when Kingsway stores were operating along the Marina on Lagos Island, a gentleman strolled into the store and picked some few items from the shelves and headed towards his car. Then, somebody accosted him and accused him of not paying for the items. I thought the man was going to counter the allegation, but I was surprised to see that he became speechless. There and then, he was taken back into the store and was thoroughly beaten for this offence. I was amazed how they got to know that he did not pay for the items. It was later, I discovered that some gadgets were installed at strategic corners of the store to detect such pilferers. It is exactly in this manner that everything we do in this world is clearly seen by God.

What we are looking at in this chapter is entitled, "The white throne judgement," and our first text is taken from Revelation 2:11-15 which says:

"And I saw a great white throne, and him that sat on it, from whose face the earth and the heaven fled away and there was found no place for them, and I saw the dead, small and great, stand before God and the books were opened; and another book was opened, which is the book of life; and the dead were judged out of those things which were written in the books, according to their works. And the sea gave up the dead which were in it; and death and hell delivered up the dead which were in them. And they were judged according to their works. And, death and hell were cast into the lake of fire. This is the second death. And whosoever was not found written in the book of life was cast into the lake of fire." This is the last judgement. .

Many people are committing atrocities for which if God decides to punish them they cannot bear the commensurate punishment. For example, imagine when only one person takes the lives of twenty people by shooting them down. What adequate punishment can be commensurate to that kind of wickedness? This is why we often emphasize in this ministry that salvation is an individual affair, it is not a collective thing. There is nothing like family salvation and nobody can rely on the fact that he comes from a Christian home as an alternative for salvation. Each person will have to stand for himself and give his own account before God.

Be Prepared

It is futile hope if one relies on the fact that one's father is an apostle. It is false hope if you hang on to the fact that you are a deacon or deaconess. If you anchor the assurance of your salvation on being a most high reverend gentleman, you are wasting your time. The Bible says, whosoever (it can be any person) whose name was not found written in that book, is cast into the lake of fire. This is referring to literal and visible fire.

On that day, before the great white throne, everybody will discover that it is going to be a personal trial in the court of God. It will be the greatest trial ever, now and in the world to come. That is why the Bible describes it as great! It is also going to be a white trial and as we know, white represents the righteousness and justice of God. All wicked persons that have ever lived will be there, from Adam to the present day. God will issue the decree of the trial and judgement whilst Jesus will execute it. But then, our own concern is not the story and description of the event. The question is where will you be? We do sing,
"In my father's house, there are many mansions there... Happy, happy we shall be. He went there to prepare a place for us..."

What happens if a person does not have accommodation

Be Prepared

there? What happens if they transfer a person's accommodation? And what happens if the person who went away and promised to come and take you home says, "No I am not taking you there!" What happens when this wicked, old and smelling world glues a person down here such that the person cannot go during the rapture?

We are told that, "Books shall be opened and another book shall be opened. This means that the number of books that will be opened cannot be less than three, and I am certain that one of them will be the Holy Bible. The second book, I am equally sure will be the Book of life whilst the third one will be God's diary where things are recorded. The Book of life will be checked to see those whose names are there, those whose names are not there and those whose names were there before but were later removed. You may ask "Is that possible?" O yes! Exodus 32:33 says,

"And the Lord said unto Moses, whosoever; hath sinned against me, him will I blot out of my book."

You can see vividly that there is no sense in being married to sin, it would only lead you to hell. There are a lot of "Sanctified sinners" and "Christian sinners" all over who have a form of godliness but are worse than witches. Some people's names were formerly in the Book of life, but when they decided to backslide, their names were removed. So, if you resort to telling stories of your past exploits for God and you are not up and doing at present, that is backsliding. It is a state of backsliding if you are not in the place where God wants you to be or doing what He wants you to do. It is not only when you completely leave your faith that you have backslidden,

The Bible says the book shall be opened to check whether people lived their lives inside or outside God. Next, God's diary shall be opened too, to cross check the record of sins people have committed. In the olden days, what the Jews understood as books were different from our modern day books. They knew books in the forms of parchments and scrolls just like our modern day cassettes and they often unfolded and spread them whenever they wanted to read from them. The books shall be spread in his manner on the day of judgement, and what everybody may have done will be read out from them. This will confirm what Jesus said that, "All the things that were said under the roof shall later be proclaim on the housetop."

Be Prepared

Sometime ago, a woman brought her husband to my office. She complained that he was fond of deserting their home and running after women. She said as a result, he had been suffering from diabetes and hypertension. She warned me to talk to him to behave. Then I asked the man what the problem was. He replied that because he was sponsoring some women to foreign countries, his wife became jealous. Then I asked the man if he was a Christian, he answered and said that he was the chairman of the building committee in his church. I said, "Sir, you are just a contractor, building a house for them but not a part of them." That is the truth. There are many people like that who come to church and contribute their money towards church progress, but are far from the Lord. People like that are not heaven-bound because they are not doing the will of the Father, Jesus said, "The first shall be the last;" He did not say "may" but "shall and this implies a certainty.

Some people may be boasting of being the first now, but at the end of the day, harlots and sinners would be sitting with Abraham and they would not be there. When He says, "I know ye not," they will ask, "What do you mean Lord? We worked miracles in your name and distributed tracts." And He will say, "You did all these things in sin, ye workers of iniquity, depart from me!" Therefore, I urge you to close your eyes and pray like this, "That terrible voice of 'depart from me' will not be directed at me, in the name of Jesus."

The great judgement has now started and the court is in session as we have read in our main text. God is seated, and there is no lawyer at the white throne judgement. All the archangels and angels are in attendance. The face of the Judge is fearful to look at! Before, He came smiling, and said, "Let children come unto me." He came in a gentle form, went about seeking the lost. But now, the day of His wrath has come and He is not ready to beam any smile. He once came and died on the cross, but now, He has turned the cross into a flaming sword. It is a fearful scene.

The Bible says, heaven and earth will fly away because they cannot withstand His face of wrath. The face of the Judge will be dreadful and terrible. The whole of heaven will be in attendance, millions and millions of people, great and small including the school girls who fold extra dresses in their bags in order to patronize boyfriends after school hours. Then there will be this great silence and the dead will begin to receive their judgement "both small and great sinners, all the fornicators and adulterers."

Be Prepared

I remember the story of a doctor who died many years ago. Immediately he gave up the ghost, he saw himself being dragged away by an unknown personality. He initially kept quiet thinking that he was being escorted into glory, but very soon he started to feel a terrible heat! On sensing danger, he started to protest to the person dragging him that he could not belong to hell as a child of God, and as they were about to throw him into the fire, a voice sounded, "Release him!" And he was released immediately. But suddenly, the devil surfaced and told God that He did not possess the right to take him to heaven because in spite of being free from all sins, he was still guilty of fornication of the heart. God agreed that the devil was correct, but insisted that He would not allow him to go to hell either, because of his wife who had been praying for him. God therefore sent back this doctor to the world with what he had seen, fresh in his memory. As a consequence, the doctor abandoned his profession and started going about to people with a message that hell is real! It will be a large gathering.

All those who commit abortions including those with various acts of sexual perversion will be there. All liars shall be there. All the thieves who are either stealing with their hands or with their pens shall be there. All the clever drunkards who pretend to be quiet and avoid disturbing people so that they would not be suspected as drunkards shall be made known that day. The dead shall come from both the sea and all the rivers. The headquarters of the queen of the coast shall be closed down. Battle fields and graveyards shall release their dead. All cemeteries will be a beehive of activities. All those things that some people ignored or despised will be duly accounted for on that great day. There will be no way of escape! They will say unto the mountains, fall on us! But it will be too late. It will dawn on them that every minute detail of their lives was recorded.

All the failures and neglected opportunities will be put down in the book. All those long forgotten sins will be written down. All the carefully concealed sins shall be made manifest. Everyone in the universe will listen and be dumbfounded at the terrible revelation that people have seen. That is why a song writer says, "Jesus is coming so happy day He goes further to say, "Not everybody will rejoice that day". The ball is in your court, you can decide to participate in the joy of the Lord.

The church is in a sad state in these last days. We are often pleased to be addressed as loving sons of God etc, but majority of us do not like being called soldiers. This is because the word "soldier" connotes violence. But the truth is that, one day, we will single-handedly stand before the throne of God.

The question is, when you stand before the throne of God, what will you say? God is ever ready to save all those who come to Him. He is equally ready to show mercy to those who are serious with what He has committed into their hands. What is the purpose of God's judgement?

The purpose of God's judgement is fourfold:

1. **To give every man a fair trial before condemnation.** The principle of justice demands that both sides be given a fair hearing. If the judges of this world follow 'the process of fair hearing, how much more God.

2. To judge the secrets of men. Romans 2:16 says, *"In the day when God shall judge the secrets of men by Jesus Christ, according to my gospel."* This explains why we warn people to get out of secret cults, familiar spirits and witchcraft societies. But some remain adamant, refusing to quit. The day of judgement is coming. All those stolen things that you are cleverly hiding shall be judged. Imagine someone putting a nice satin material on top of a stolen underwear.

Even though people may admire your outfit, but as far as God is concerned, you are a thief. We look at the outside but God looks at the inside.

3. To judge all the spoken idle words. Matthew 12:36-37 says, "But I say unto you, that every idle word that men shall speak, they shall give account thereof in the day of judgement. For by thy words thou shall be justified, and by thy words thou shalt be condemned."

All the words you have ever spoken shall be judged. Therefore, you should be careful what you say with your mouth. If you cannot control your tongue, you will face the risk of condemnation on the day of judgement. Remember, all your works, thoughts and actions shall be judged. It is therefore wise to pray that this judgement does pot come upon us unawares. The task before us now is to prove to God that the lives we are living will qualify us for heaven. My friend, a day is coming by and by and I do not want you to read this kind of message only to continue in your cold and sluggish Christian life. God will not excuse you on the basis that you have been long in the Christian faith, neither will He excuse you on the fact that you are a pastor or a minister.

Be Prepared

All the former believers who are falling from grace and yet pretends as if they are still on fire will discover their folly that day. You may be hiding from men but you cannot hide from God. There are only two ways; the broad way that leads to hell and the narrow way that leads to glory. There are also two kinds of people; the sheep and the goats. There are only two deaths, the death of the righteous and the death of the wicked. We have only two futures; the kingdom of heaven and hell fire. The choice is yours. It is you who will decide where you are going to spend your eternity. As for me, I made a personal decision long ago that I am not going to hell fire. In the same manner, be resolute that you will not allow the enemy to lead you to perdition.

God will definitely pick His own when all these things begin to happen. That is why He warns, "Behold, I sent you forth as sheep amongst wolves." You are supposed to survive there because sheep dwelling amidst wolves must possess certain things " that would prevent wolves from eating them up.

Beloved, consider the number of years you have wasted and know for sure that you may not have up to that number of years to live again. That is why the Bible says, "Whatsoever your hands findeth to do, do it with all your might." (Eccls. 9 : 10) Also, a song writer says, "Lord I care not for riches, neither silver nor gold, I would make sure of heaven. I would enter the fold. In the book of thy kingdom with its pages so fair. Tell me, Jesus, my Saviour is my name written there?" Are you sure your name is in the book of life? If you are not sure yet, you better put your house in order and be sure today. I am not asking you whether you have been confirmed or whether you are speaking in tongues.

It is a fact that many tongue speakers will land in hell fire. They will ask, "Was it not in your name that we prophesied? Many prophets also will find themselves in hell fire including many miracle workers. They too will ask, "Did we not do many miracles in your name?" How can it be said that in spite of your going up and down, singing today, teaching tomorrow, distributing tracts and being a member of prayer warrior group, you suddenly find yourself on the same seat with the children of the devil laughing you to scorn in hell? "

There are a lot of people who have been struggling with bad habits for years, yet they keep on pampering them even though they know they are bad. How long will you keep pampering and defending your enemy? Do you want to say before the Lord that the blood of Jesus is no longer powerful or that the Holy Spirit is no longer available to help you? Did you not hear sound teachings? What do you want to say? You want to say that you do not know that all these things are bad? May be you have gone round many churches but you still remain where you are after many years. Do you think that God will be satisfied with your life? Talk to the Lord to show you the area where you need to make corrections today.

PRAYER POINTS
1. Let the Holy Spirit fill me afresh, in the name of Jesus.
2. Father Lord, incubate me with the fire of the Holy Ghost, in Jesus name
3. Oh Lord, catapult my spiritual life to the mountain top, in Jesus name.
4. Father Lord, fill me with spiritual gifts, in the name of Jesus.
5. Let every unbroken area of my life, be broken, in the name of Jesus.
6. Lord open my understanding concerning the scriptures, in Jesus name.
7. O Lord, uphold my faith, in the name of Jesus.
8. Father Lord, make me hunger and thirst for righteousness, in Jesus name.
9. Lord, release the Pentecostal tongue of fire to burn away all spiritual filthiness in my life, in the name of Jesus.

MFM and The Author

Dr.D.K. Olukoya is the General Overseer of the Mountain of Fire and Miracles Ministries and The Battle Cry Christian Ministries.

The Mountain of Fire and Miracles Ministries Headquarters is the largest single Christian congregation in Africa with attendance of over 120,000 in single meetings.

MFM is a full gospel ministry devoted to the revival of Apostolic signs, Holy Ghost Fireworks, miracles and the unlimited demonstration of the power of God to deliver to the uttermost. Absolute holiness within and without as spiritual insecticide and pre-requisite for heaven is openly taught.

MFM is a do-it-yourself Gospel Ministry, where your hands are trained to wage war and your fingers to do battles.
Dr. Olukoya holds a first class honours degree in Micro-biology from the University of Lagos and a PhD in Molecular Genetics from the University of Reading, United Kingdom. As a researcher, he has over seventy scientific publications to his credit.

Anointed by God. Dr. Olukoya is a prophet, evangelist, teacher and preacher of the Word. His life and that of his wife, Shade and their son Elijah Toluwani are living proofs that all power belongs to God.

Published by:
The PRESSHOUSE
MOUNTAIN OF FIRE AND MIRACLES MINISTRIES
13, Olasimbo Street, Off Olumo Road (near UNILAG 2nd Gate),Onike.
P. O. Box 2990, Sabo, Tel: 867439, 868766, Lagos. Nigeria.
E-mail: mfm@micro.com.ng mfm@nigol.net.ng Website: www.mountain-of-fire.com

www.ingramcontent.com/pod-product-compliance
Lightning Source LLC
Chambersburg PA
CBHW071309060426
42444CB00034B/1751